HAGGAI,
ZECHARIAH,
MALACHI

Living Word BIBLE STUDIES

HAGGAI, ZECHARIAH, MALACHI

Pointing to the Promised King

KATHLEEN BUSWELL NIELSON

P&R PUBLISHING

P.O. BOX 817 • PHILLIPSBURG • NEW JERSEY 08865-0817

If you find this Bible study helpful, consider writing a review online
—or contact P&R at editorial@prpbooks.com with your comments.
We'd love to hear from you.

ISBN: 978-1-62995-832-3 (pbk)
ISBN: 978-1-62995-833-0 (ePub)

Printed in the United States of America

CONTENTS

A PERSONAL WORD
FROM KATHLEEN

In preparing this study on three postexilic prophets, I read again this "personal word" written years ago for the first of my studies, a guide for the book of Proverbs. Often when we read words we wrote a long time ago, we cringe—and we're anxious to make changes! I'm happy to find that these words stand. That is only because they are about the Living Word that never changes and never fails. May we followers of the Lord Jesus never stop hearing and loving God's Word, by the power of the Spirit, and may we keep walking in its light, to the end.

I began to write these Bible studies for the women in my own church group at College Church in Wheaton, Illinois. Under the leadership of Kent and Barbara Hughes, the church and that Bible study aimed to proclaim without fail the good news of the Word of God. What a joy, in that study and in many since, to see lives changed by the work of the Word, by the Spirit, for the glory of Christ.

In our Bible study group, we were looking for curriculum that would lead us into the meat of the Word and teach us how to take it in, whole Bible books at a time—the way they are given to us in Scripture. Finally, one of our leaders said, "Kathleen—how

about if you just write it!" And so began one of the most joy-
ful projects of my life: the writing of studies intended to help
unleash the Word of God in people's lives. The writing began
during a busy stage of my life—with three lively young boys and
always a couple of college English courses to teach—but through
that stage and every busy one since, a serious attention to studying the Bible has helped keep me focused, growing, and alive in
the deepest ways. The Word of God will do that. If there's life
and power in these studies, it is simply the life and power of
the Scriptures to which they point. It is ultimately the life and
power of the Savior who shines through all the Scriptures from
beginning to end. How we need this life, in the midst of every
busy and non-busy stage of our lives!

I don't think it is just the English teacher in me that leads me
to this conclusion about our basic problem in Bible study these
days: we've forgotten how to *read*! We're so used to fast food that
we think we should be able to drive by the Scriptures periodi-
cally and pick up some easily digestible truths that someone else
has wrapped up neatly for us. We've disowned that process of
careful reading . . . observing the words . . . seeing the shape of a
book and a passage . . . asking questions that take us into the text
rather than away from it . . . digging into the Word and letting it
speak! Through such a process, guided by the Spirit, the Word
of God truly feeds our souls. Here's my prayer: that, by means
of these studies, people would be further enabled to read the
Scriptures profitably and thereby find life and nourishment in
them, as we are each meant to do.

In all the busy stages of life and writing, I have been continu-
ally surrounded by pastors, teachers, and family who encourage
and help me in this work, and for that I am grateful. The most
wonderful guidance and encouragement come from my husband,
Niel, whom I thank and for whom I thank God daily.

May God use these studies to lift up Christ and his Word,
for his glory!

INTRODUCTION

Reading the last three Old Testament prophets is, in one sense, like peering into the deepest, darkest layer of salvation history.

The people to whom these prophets spoke had a magnificent history behind them. We will review that history in Lesson One, remembering God's promise to bless this seed of Abraham and through them to bring blessing to all the families of the earth. God indeed blessed them, growing them into a great nation in the promised land. But they squandered that blessing, turned from their Lord God, and suffered the consequences of their sin as they were divided, conquered, and exiled from their land.

When Haggai, Zechariah, and Malachi bring God's word to this people, they address only a remnant of weak, struggling Jews, servants of the Persian Empire, allowed to return to Jerusalem to rebuild a broken-down temple and city. God's people still have God's promises, but they're peering into the dark to see them.

Reading the last three Old Testament prophets is, in another sense, like seeing the brightest light shining out of darkness.

These three postexilic prophets are the closest of all the prophets to the fulfillment to come four hundred years later: the birth of Jesus—the promised seed of Abraham, the King in the line of David, the Savior who would finally and fully deliver his people. These prophecies lean far forward, reaching for the next thing to happen in salvation history. We will see Jesus Christ shining through the words of these writers who spoke from God to a poor and needy people looking for a king.

We have the history of this period in the books of Ezra and Nehemiah. But what a gift to have the writings of the prophets, words given by God to speak directly to his people. As God's people now, through faith in his Son who came, we also take these words to heart—for we, too, are a poor and needy people in many ways. We have seen the King in his first advent, the Savior who came to bear our sin and suffer God's wrath in our place to save us, forever. We celebrate his resurrection and his ascension into heaven—and now we wait for him. We, too, long to see the King, this time when he comes again.

Our aim in this study is to understand the words of these prophets first in their own context, as they addressed the remnant of Jews who returned to their land. We will ask how these words challenged and encouraged God's people then. And we will ask how these words continue to challenge and encourage us believers now. For these God-breathed words are alive and active, still sharper than a two-edged sword as they by God's Spirit penetrate our hearts and reveal the Lord to us. In a world so full of people and nations who reject the God of the Bible, we are indeed still a weak remnant—but a quickly growing one, and one (as these prophets predicted) bringing together believers from all the nations of the world to worship the King of the whole earth.

Each lesson in this study begins with an introduction that clarifies the theme of the book and the section to be covered. To read these three books in ten weeks does not allow for detailed study; the aim is to read them carefully, to grasp their basic meaning and structure, and to begin to let them pierce our hearts as the Spirit helps us hear and understand. These prophecies are unified literary masterpieces; we do well to take them in first as whole books, before we isolate too many individual words and verses for complex study. Taking in the larger flow, we will aim to grasp how the books hold together and what major themes they develop from beginning to end. When we're done and we say "Haggai" or "Zechariah" or "Malachi," I hope we will say each name with a clear and satisfying sense of just what each book is all about—its essence.

There are no "commentary" sections in the study; necessary and helpful commentary is embedded in the questions that lead through the biblical text section by section. I have included a short list of commentaries that have been helpful to me and that may enrich your study of these books at some point. First and foremost, do read and reread the biblical text. At the start of each lesson, it will be helpful to read the whole section covered that week. Before beginning the study—and again afterward—it will be helpful to read through the books in their entirety.

When we're done, I pray these postexilic prophets will seem like bright lights to us, shining out of the darkness, lighting the way toward the promised King.

Lesson 1
(Introduction; Hag. 1:1–15)

GOD SPEAKS TO THE REMNANT

In Lesson One, our aim is to set the three final Old Testament prophets in their biblical and historical context, and to begin our acquaintance with Haggai. The wonder of the prophets is that God kept on sending his word to his people, throughout their sin-filled journey, which would finally culminate in the coming of Jesus the promised Redeemer King. The specific message of Haggai is that *the all-powerful Lord commands and helps his people not to falter in worshiping him to the very end, when through their line of promise God's glory will be revealed.*

Haggai 1 shows us a remnant of God's people who *have* faltered in worshiping him—just as his people today often do. They have ceased rebuilding the Jerusalem temple, the place and the means of worship God had provided. We'll see that God graciously sends his word, calling them to see their error and mend their ways (vv. 1–11), and that with God's empowerment they listen and respond (vv. 12–15). After all the Old Testament stories of God's disobedient people, what a joy to read an account in which they hear and obey the voice of the Lord!

Reading these Old Testament prophets, we New Testament believers aim first to understand their messages in their original contexts. We also aim to see how these messages point ahead to Jesus Christ, the fulfillment of all God's promises (2 Cor. 1:20). As we read of the biological seed of Abraham, we joyfully count ourselves part of the family of God's chosen people by faith in Christ our Savior (Gal. 3:7–9, 29). The Bible's story is our story, revealing the triune God from beginning to end. These prophets called God's people to return to him and trust him fully; we today do well to open our ears to their God-breathed call.

Day One—God and His People

Let's remember who these people are to whom Haggai, Zechariah, and Malachi prophesy: they are descendants of Abraham. The whole story begins in the book of Genesis, which tells of God's creation of a perfect world and a perfect man and woman made to commune with him (Gen. 1–2). But sin invaded God's creation, as the first man and woman disobeyed God's command (Gen. 3). The Bible's early chapters tell how the world was filled with sinful rebellion against God, and how God punished this rebellion with a great flood, saving only Noah and his family, for "Noah found favor in the eyes of the Lord" (Gen. 6:8). From the line of Noah came Abraham.

1. In Genesis 12:1–7, what promises does God make to Abraham, and how does Abraham respond?

2. Read Nehemiah 9:6-25, part of the historical summary given in a prayer of God's people looking back on what the Lord had done for them. List some of the ways in which God did indeed bless the descendants of Abraham.

3. As Abraham's descendants established a great kingdom in the land God gave them, God channeled his promises through the line of King David. Read God's covenant with David in 2 Samuel 7:12–17. Then look briefly through Matthew 1:1–17; 2:1–2; 4:17; 21:1–9; Colossians 1:11–13; Hebrews 1:1–8. Sum up God's great promise to David, and how the New Testament shows its final fulfillment.

4. The wait for that promised king was long and hard. Throughout the Old Testament, God's people kept turning away from the Lord. The kingdom under David split, and eventually both parts were conquered and taken into exile. The last place to fall (in 586 BC) was Jerusalem, the capital city of the southern kingdom of Judah. Read the final heartbreaking account in 2 Chronicles 36:15–21 and summarize the main characters and the main actions. *Note: The "Chaldeans" are Babylonians, who overthrew Jerusalem.*

5. As we read in Chronicles, the prophet Jeremiah foretold that the exile from Jerusalem would last seventy years (see Jer. 25:11–14; 29:10–14)—and then the Babylonians who conquered God's people would themselves be conquered. The process of exile began as early as 605 BC, well before Jerusalem's fall. In 539 BC, the Babylonians *were* conquered, by the Persians—and in the next few years groups of Jewish exiles began to return to their land, according to the decree of Persian king Cyrus (all in God's plan; see Isa. 45:1, 13). How does Ezra's account of the first return shape our perspective on King Cyrus and on all this history (Ezra 1:1–5)?

DAY TWO—GOD SPEAKS TO HIS PEOPLE

1. In the beginning, God spoke directly with Adam and Eve, and also with others like Cain and Abel (Gen. 4:1–7) and Noah (Gen. 7:1–5). Soon the Lord called prophets: ones to whom God gives his word to give to others. What similarities do you notice among the early prophets Moses (Ex. 34:29–33), Samuel (1 Sam. 3:19–21), and Elijah (1 Kings 21:17–19)?

2. The "writing prophets" came during the decline, fall, and rebuilding of the kingdom. What similarities do you notice in these representative opening verses: Jeremiah 1:1–2; Amos 1:1–3; Micah 1:1–2? *Note: The writing prophets are called "major" and "minor" simply depending on the length of their books; our three postexilic prophets are "minor."*

3. Do a quick read-through of the book of Haggai, marking or listing the multiple phrases indicating that this book is the word of the Lord. Jot down a few initial impressions and thoughts on this first reading.

4. Read 2 Peter 1:16–21. What truths can we know for sure concerning the prophecies of Scripture? Stop to pray and thank God that he speaks to us, ultimately through his Son. Ask him to help us see his Son shining at the heart of these God-breathed prophecies given to the Jewish remnant through whose seed the promised King would come.

Day Three—Consider Your Ways
(Hag. 1:1–11)

We've seen the general historical context of the Jewish remnant that returned to its land by decree of the Persian emperor. Haggai 1:1 gives specific context: the events of this book took place in the second year of the third Persian ruler, King Darius—520 BC, about eighteen years after King Cyrus's proclamation and the exiles' return to Jerusalem to rebuild the temple. *Note: This early group of returned exiles was led primarily by two men, whom Haggai addresses repeatedly: Judah's governor Zerubbabel the son of Shealtiel, and the high priest Joshua (or "Jeshua") the son of Jehozadak (1:1, 12, 14; 2:2, 4, 21, 23). Governor Zerubbabel was a descendant of King David (see Matt. 1:12–13), and Joshua was a descendant of Aaron the high priest. Another early governor, Sheshbazzar the "prince of Judah," is also mentioned in Ezra 1:8 and 5:14–16, but Zerubbabel emerges as the leader and governor during these events.*

1. Read Haggai 1:1–2 and Ezra 3:1–4:5 to grasp the situation of the returned exiles under Haggai's ministry. How far had the people progressed in rebuilding the temple, and what kinds of discouragements and excuses had stopped them? (In what ways can you identify with these discouragements and excuses?)

2. The temple was the place of God's presence, where priests offered sacrifices for the people's sin, mediating and providing access to the Lord they worshiped in the way he had commanded them. Read about the dedication of the Jerusalem temple in 1 Kings 7:51–8:21. Then comment on the significance of the temple to God's Old Testament people.

3. In light of the significance of the temple, consider what God says in Haggai 1:3–6, 9–11 about their neglecting it. What do God's words reveal about the nature of their wrong and of the consequences they are suffering?

4. Let's pause to "consider our ways" (Hag. 1:5, 7) as believers today.

   a. We don't come to a building with priests and sacrifices in our time of salvation history, when the promised offspring of Abraham has come. Read John 2:13–22; Hebrews 10:11–14, 19–25; 1 Peter 2:4–5. What did Jesus do for us that all those priests and sacrifices could not? How and where do Christians worship God today?

   b. Suggest a few ways we followers of Jesus are tempted to focus insatiably on our own households rather than the household of God.

5. Finally, note the strong command at the heart of this passage (Hag. 1:8), and note God's stated purpose. What can we learn here about God and about ourselves?

DAY FOUR—STIRRED UP TO OBEY (HAG. 1:12–15)

1. Read Haggai 1:12–15. First, focus on *the Lord's role* in the ensuing response. What aspects of that role emerge in the text?

2. Now, focus on *the people's role* in responding. What different aspects of their response can you notice, and why is each one so crucial?

3. As we saw, this scene is part of a long story of God's dealings with his people. In light of Haggai 1:12–15, what connecting words and themes do you find in the following verses?

   a. Exodus 33:12–16

b. Deuteronomy 6:1–3

c. Joshua 1:5–7

d. Isaiah 41:8–10

4. We believers are part of the same story, with the same God
   at work. How do Matthew 1:21–23 and John 14:15–17
   help us even more fully understand God's promise "I am
   with you"? What words and phrases stand out to you in
   these verses, and why?

5. Look back over Haggai 1 to find the name for God repeatedly used: the "LORD of hosts" (as in the commander of a great army). How does the emphasis of this name deepen the impact of Haggai's message?

DAY FIVE—REVIEW AND REFLECT

1. At the beginning of this lesson we said the specific message of Haggai is that *the all-powerful Lord commands and helps his people not to falter in worshiping him to the very end, when through their line of promise God's glory will be revealed.* Briefly explain what parts of this summary statement Haggai 1 has brought to light.

2. Haggai 1 moves us as people of God to "consider our ways," for we know what it is to falter in following our Lord. In what specific ways might this prophet's words convict us to turn from busying ourselves with our own households, and turn to worshiping and serving in the household of God, for the glory of Christ our Savior? What might this look like for you?

3. In what ways might we be tempted to apply this chapter moralistically, as simply a condemnation of our badness and a demand for our goodness? What might be the results? What in this chapter keeps us from that kind of application?

4. Meditate on Jesus's words in Matthew 6:25–34. What does he tell his followers not to do? What does he tell them to do, and how might you begin to do it? (Suggestion: Focus your answer on the righteous King Jesus.)

5. Let's end with looking up to the Lord of hosts, who is the initiator and prime actor of this story. Write a summary list of what this chapter shows us about him. Then write and/or speak a prayer thanking him for who he is and how he watches over his people through each chapter of their stories, for his redemptive purposes in Christ Jesus.

Notes for Lesson 1

Lesson 2 (Hag. 2:1-23)

GOD PROMISES GLORY
AND BLESSING

In Haggai 1, we saw the returned exiles respond to God's call to resume work on rebuilding the Jerusalem temple. Now in Haggai 2, almost a month into their labor, they are discouraged again—and God mercifully speaks again. The main message of Haggai continues and expands, as we see the all-powerful Lord *commanding and helping his people not to falter in worshiping him to the very end, when through their line of promise God's glory will be revealed.* In the second chapter, the promise of glory shines brilliantly in the midst of hard, discouraging work.

The original temple had been burned down by the Babylonians sixty-six years earlier, in 586 BC, when the kingdom of Judah fell. Only some of the older ones among the remnant would be able to remember the magnificent temple built by King Solomon—glorious in its physical structure and even more in its filling with God's very presence. It seemed now as if the glory was lost. This was a hard time to hope. And this is why it is good for us to read this book, especially in times when we struggle to persevere in hope.

In God's word sent through Haggai, his people receive a promise of even greater glory to be revealed in the Lord's temple. No more would the temple be at the center of an earthly kingdom; God's promises of a king in the line of David point to a kingdom even greater—as the Scriptures show us.

DAY ONE—GOD SPEAKS INTO DISCOURAGEMENT (HAG. 2:1–5)

1. Read Haggai 2:1–23 in preparation for this lesson, and then focus on Haggai 2:1–3 to review the details of time (recall Hag. 1:1, 15) and characters (see Lesson One). What is the effect of hearing the various characters named and addressed so specifically? *Note: The twenty-first day of the seventh month would fall during the Feast of Tabernacles, when the people celebrated God's deliverance of Israel from Egypt and his care for them in the wilderness.*

2. After several weeks of rebuilding and seeing the temple take shape, the people are discouraged again. Why? Before responding, recall 1 Kings 8:1–11 (the original temple's dedication, which occurred also during the Feast of Tabernacles) and skim through Ezekiel 10:3–22, the mysterious vision of an earlier prophet who spoke even as Jerusalem fell to the Babylonians and who told of God's glory departing from the temple.

3. In what ways might we as the people of God today identify with this sort of discouragement, looking back to
   much better-seeming periods of blessing and spiritual
   life? And how can we be encouraged by God's acknowledgment of this perspective (Hag. 2:3)?

4. Now we're ready for the heart of this message to God's
   discouraged people. First, in preparation for Day Two,
   just read and relish Haggai 2:4–9. Begin to observe by
   listing the various commands given by God in verses
   4–5. What is the tone and effect of these commands,
   particularly as they follow verse 3?

DAY TWO—THE GLORY OF GOD WITH US
(HAG. 2:4–9)

1. Attached to God's commands is the promise of God's *presence*, affirmed in Haggai 1:13 and reiterated here. Write down the various truths Haggai 2:4–5 can teach us about God's presence with his people. For background, first read Exodus 19:1–6; 29:38–46—where God makes covenant promises to his people at Mount Sinai after the exodus from Egypt, as he gives them his law and the ceremonial system of worship that would allow them to come into his presence through priestly mediation and sacrifices.

2. "My Spirit remains in your midst," says the Lord (Hag. 2:5). From the beginning, God has worked through his Spirit on the earth. It is true that the indwelling Spirit was sent to believers in a new way following Christ's death, resurrection, and ascension (Acts 2:1–21). But this third person of the Trinity, the Holy Spirit, has always been present and active. For example, read Genesis 1:2; Numbers 27:18; Isaiah 63:10–14; and Zechariah 4:6. Note several phrases that stand out to you.

3. We saw what God commands his people to do. Now, in Haggai 2:6–9, list all the "I wills"—the things God says he will do. How do these verses emphasize God's sovereign power to do what he says he will do?

4. Haggai 2:6–9 reaches far back and far forward, showing God's mighty hand shaping history for his redemptive purposes. The shaking of the natural world foreseen in verse 6 recalls language describing the exodus (see Ps. 77:16–19)—and God will so act again on behalf of his people. Certainly he will act to protect this remnant. But the cosmic scope of the language asks us to look ahead to the climactic moments of salvation's story.

   a. What climactic deliverance shook the world at the cross and the empty grave (Matt. 27:51; 28:2)?

b. According to 2 Peter 3:8–13, what kind of shaking is still to come, when the risen Christ returns? What is Peter's perspective on the timing of these events?

c. How does Hebrews 12:18–28 speak about God's shaking of the heavens and earth, using Haggai's words?

5. Haggai 2:7–9 tells how God will fill this house with even greater glory than before—and with peace. How do the following verses shed light on the fulfillment of Haggai's words? Read all, but select one to use in writing your answer.

   • Isaiah 2:1–4

- John 1:14; 2:18–21
- Revelation 21:22–27
- Ephesians 2:13–22

Day Three—Blessing for a Sinful People (Hag. 2:10–19)

1. Three months into rebuilding, at the time for planting new seed, God sends two final messages through this prophet. First, read Haggai 2:10–19, where some law-related questions to the priests point to the power of sin to contaminate all aspects of life. Left to themselves, this sinful people (like all of us) could not please God with any of their works or offerings (v. 14). What was at the heart of the people's sin, according to verse 17? How did their neglect of the temple rebuilding relate to that sin?

2. God says before the rebuilding began, he sent economic hardship to turn his sinful people to himself—but they did not respond. What are we learning about God here? In Haggai 2:10-17, what attributes of God stand out, and why?

3. The Lord mercifully calls his people to "consider" (Hag. 2:15, 18): to turn their hearts to his words. They have indeed been responding, placing stone upon stone in the temple (v. 15)—and God steps in at a season of sowing and promises blessing like they haven't seen for a while (v. 19). So, consider: How is the temple rebuilding key to solving the problem of "uncleanness" in this people and every work of their hands? How is the temple connected to the blessing?

4. Think back to the overwhelming glory promised in Haggai 2:6–9. What shall we make of the transition to this message a couple months later—seemingly much more mundane, focused on the crops? For these struggling subjects of the Persian Empire, both past and future glory must have seemed far away. Why would this message be crucial for God's people as they persevered in the ongoing work of planting crops and rebuilding the temple?

5. In the midst of all our building and planting, as God's people today we must stop often, individually and corporately, to turn to God and consider what he has done for us in his glorious Son. Left to ourselves, we would have nothing to offer or to please God. Take a moment to think on the Lord Jesus, who "bore our sins in his body on the tree" (1 Peter 2:24). Run to him, our temple. By grace, through faith in Christ, we find the blessing of forgiveness and the promise of glory, life as part of the body of Christ in God's presence now and forever.

DAY FOUR—BLESSING THROUGH DAVID'S LINE
(HAG. 2:20–23)

1. Haggai's final message comes on the same day as the previous one; the simple promise of blessing (Hag. 2:19) is wonderfully expanded in the final verses. But the message is finally for Zerubbabel alone, this descendant of King David in whose line God had promised an eternal King. First, consider verses 20–22.

   a. What is the sum and the tone of this part of the message?

   b. Like verses 6–9, how do these verses echo God's past actions in the exodus (see Ex. 15:1–4)? How does this correspondence help us understand which kingdoms and nations will be destroyed by God, and why?

c. These verses point forward through layers of human history to the very end. How do Psalm 46:6–11 and Revelation 11:15–19 similarly describe God's final power over the nations that oppose him and his people?

2. But why does this message come specifically to Zerubbabel? In what ways is he highlighted in Haggai 2:23? Before responding, read Jeremiah 22:24–27. (Read also Psalm 89:3–4, and recall Matthew 1:12–13.) *Note: Jehoiachin (or "Jeconiah," or "Coniah") was the last descendant of David to rule as king in Judah; he was deposed and exiled by the Babylonians. A signet ring was a symbol of his kingly authority—taken away.*

3. Zerubbabel represents the surety of God's promise to bring an eternal King in David's line. That King is the one who will accomplish this deliverance. God's covenant stands. Think of the comfort this brought to this Jewish remnant. What related truths does Psalm 2 show us about the promised King?

4. Zerubbabel points our eyes forward to the returning King Jesus, who on the day of his return will be both risen Savior of his people and final judge of all who have rejected him. Spend some moments thanking God for the sure hope found in our eternal King and praying for those who do not have this hope. How do Haggai's final four verses impress on you the urgency of sharing this hope?

DAY FIVE—REVIEW AND REFLECT

1. At the beginning of this study we said the specific message of Haggai is that *the all-powerful Lord commands and helps his people not to falter in worshiping him to the very end, when through their line of promise God's glory will be revealed.* Briefly explain what parts of this summary statement Haggai 2 has especially brought to light.

2. This little book has shown us a large vision—of a mighty God. Look through Haggai 2 to find the instances of the title "LORD of hosts." Why do you think this title is so often repeated? What truths has this chapter shown you about the "LORD of hosts"?

3. Think back to the central importance of the temple in this book: God would not have his house abandoned. As we've said, we believers today do not need a physical temple; Jesus has come, and by grace, through faith in his final sacrifice in our place, we draw near to God. For the body of Christ today, how would you summarize Haggai's message concerning the temple?

4. How might this book of Haggai teach you to pray? For what does this book lead you to thank God? What supplications and renewed obedience might it inspire?

5. Conclude as the book concludes: with a look forward to the Servant-King who did come in David's line, who died to save us, and who rose to reign forever with his people. Run to Jesus our temple, and worship the King.

Notes for Lesson 2

Lesson 3 (Zech. 1:1–21)

GOD IS JEALOUS
FOR JERUSALEM

We move now to the second postexilic prophet—but we don't have to move far. Zechariah's prophetic ministry began just two months after Haggai's (see Hag. 1:1; Zech. 1:1); they together brought the word of the Lord to this struggling remnant of Jews who had been allowed by the Persian ruler to return to their land and who were called to rebuild the temple in Jerusalem.

Before beginning this lesson, it will be helpful to review Lessons One and Two in order to recall the biblical background and context of this moment in redemptive history. As the Old Testament record draws to a close, we glimpse God's chosen people at a low point, having lost their great earthly kingdom because of their sinfulness—and yet still holding on to God's promises of an eternal King to come from their seed.

Through his prophets God called his people to remember his promises and to live in light of them even in hard times. Zechariah in particular *urged God's people to return to the Lord and to look in faith for the glorious plan of salvation to be accomplished through the coming King, who would restore Jerusalem in a greater way than they could imagine.* Zechariah helped them imagine, stretching their minds and hearts through visions and oracles that point ultimately to the glory of King Jesus and his eternal kingdom.

Zechariah also helps *us* imagine. We New Testament believers have seen the glory of Jesus revealed in his first coming, his death, his resurrection, and his ascension in the clouds. But we wait in faith for his coming again with all his glory revealed, to judge the nations and to dwell with his people in the new heaven and earth. Zechariah helps us long to see the King.

Day One—God Directs the Story (Overview)

1. We have seen the discouragement of the returned exiles, whose work in rebuilding the temple began and then ceased for about fifteen years—until in 520 BC Haggai and Zechariah rose up with their words from the Lord. The temple rebuilding was finally finished in 515 BC. Skim through the account in Ezra 5:1–6:18, where we see Haggai and Zechariah's joint ministry highlighted. What details emphasize God's sovereign and gracious hand at work?

2. God's raising up Haggai and Zechariah at this crucial time showed his unfailing care for his people. The name *Zechariah* means "Yahweh remembered"; our faithful Lord will never forget his people or his promises to them. Find some of Zechariah's family connections in Zechariah 1:1 and Nehemiah 12:1–5, 16; stop to thank God for his sovereign preparation and placing of leaders in the lives of his people. *Note: Zechariah is mentioned by Jesus in Matthew 23:29–36 as the final prophet who was persecuted and killed; the same kind of death of an earlier "Zechariah" is mentioned in 2 Chronicles 24:20–21, but both may well have met the same end.*

3. Let's get a sense of this book as a whole. First, after an introduction in Zechariah 1:1–6, chapters 1–6 consist of a series of nine visual revelations from the Lord, symbolic pictures given to Zechariah by an angel who interprets them for him and for the people to whom he prophesies—including us. This kind of literature is often called *apocalyptic*, which means that it unveils or reveals invisible spiritual realities, often future ones, through highly symbolic language. Skim through these chapters, glimpsing some of the pictures given and explained. What are your first impressions and questions?

4. Zechariah 7–8 comprise a middle section, with prophetic words given two years later (7:1). Here Zechariah is more direct, speaking the truth of the previous words (and the ones to come) into the realities of life and worship in Jerusalem as the people resettle and rebuild. Along with a call for justice and mercy among them come encouragement and hope that God's favor would indeed rest on them—in fact *through* them on the peoples of the earth. Skim Zechariah 8:14–23; what phrases encourage you even in this initial reading?

5. The book concludes with a contrasting section—so different that some scholars have argued for different authorship. But Zechariah is turning his attention here to God's large purposes in the world through his people; he gives two concluding "burdens" (beginning Zech. 9:1 and 12:1) that serve as oracles, prophetic messages of great and urgent import. The words reach out to offer some of the Old Testament's most vivid prophecies of the coming King, the Lord Jesus. Just look through Zechariah 9–14; for each chapter's beginning, make a note or two about the ways in which we are pointed to a sovereign God who is accomplishing his plan for Israel and for the whole earth.

DAY TWO—A GRACIOUS CALL TO RETURN
(ZECH. 1:1–6)

1. The book's overall message is well summarized by the
   opening call in Zechariah 1:2–3. What do we learn about
   the nature of our God here? Read also Jeremiah 3:12–14.

2. To understand what is involved in "returning" to the
   Lord, examine the negative example of God's rebellious
   people before the kingdom's fall and the exile (Zech.
   1:4–6a). What could the returned exiles (and what can
   we) learn from that earlier part of the story?

3. But the story did not end with God's judgment on that generation of exiles. After the exile, many repented, acknowledging that God had punished them for their sin (Zech. 1:6b; recall Ezra 5:12). In Haggai, we saw the remnant turning to follow God's words when they had turned away. Zechariah is calling for them to follow the path of repentance, continuing to take God's Word to heart.

   a. How might the temple they're rebuilding help this people return to the Lord?

   b. What does this life of repentance and returning look like now, for a follower of Jesus? See 1 John 1:5–10.

4. Reread Zechariah 1:1–6 to find the repeated name for God. How does the meaning of this name help strengthen the message of these verses? And how does this name strengthen and encourage you personally?

DAY THREE—HORSEMEN AND HORNS
(ZECH. 1:7–21)

1. Read Zechariah's first vision (Zech. 1:7–17). This is "the word of the Lord"—a vision communicated with Spirit-breathed words. At night, Zechariah sees a man on a red horse standing (pausing on the horse, it seems) at the head of a troop of riders on various-colored horses, in a grove of myrtle trees with their thick green leaves. Details in these pictures are arresting and sometimes confusing; we can't understand it all! This first rider appears to be the "angel of the LORD who was standing among the myrtle trees" (v. 11)—the one who talks with Zechariah. First, just peer into the rich, deep, colorful picture. Then consider verses 9–11. What do we learn about God from seeing this troop of angelic patrols?

2. For a people expecting God to "shake the nations" (Hag. 2:7, 21–22) and restore their kingdom, an earth "at rest" might not have sounded hopeful. In Zechariah 1:12–17, in what ways do the question and the answer evidence God's faithfulness and mercy toward his people?

3. The angel of the Lord who comforts, intercedes for, and speaks to God's people has been identified by some readers as one of the Old Testament's glimpses of the preincarnate second person of the Trinity (compare Gen. 22:11–18; Josh. 5:13–15). We might be led to think ahead to the end of the earthly story, to another vision of one sitting on a horse. Read Revelation 19:11–16; what truths are fully revealed in that horseman picture?

4. Read Zechariah 1:18–21. In this second and related vision, four horns (symbols of strength) represent nations that conquer and exile the northern and southern kingdoms. Then four craftsmen (strong workmen, perhaps with hammers or anvils) represent nations decreed to conquer the conquerors of God's people. God's sovereign hand would already have been evident in the Assyrians' conquering of the northern kingdom (722 BC), the Babylonians' subsequent conquering of the southern kingdom (586 BC), and the Persians' subsequent conquering of the Babylonians (539 BC). Even as God's power extends over all the nations, what is his ultimate aim? See Zechariah 1:14–17, Genesis 12:3, and Isaiah 2:1–4.

5. Look back through Zechariah 1. In what ways are heavenly mercies evident throughout this communication with people on earth? What is Zechariah's role and attitude as he receives God's Word? What can we learn here about how to receive God's Word?

Day Four—Receiving the Visions Today

1. If we have been joined to God's family by faith in the Lord Jesus Christ, then we are among the blessed children of Abraham (see Gal. 3:7–9, 29). We can seek and find the comfort the Lord gives to his beloved people. He is jealous for us. He has clear plans for us—and for those who oppose us (and him). Read Isaiah 45:1–13, the Lord's revelation through Isaiah that he would sovereignly direct the Persian emperor Cyrus to end the Jewish exile and commission the rebuilding in Jerusalem. What repeated truths do Isaiah and Zechariah (and other prophets) tell us about God's care for his people?

2. As we've seen, the capital city of Jerusalem with its temple on Mount Zion showed God's plan to bless and dwell with his people. God's promises for Jerusalem applied to the people rebuilding in Zechariah's day, and they reach into the future—to us now, and to a "heavenly Jerusalem" to come. What do we know about that heavenly Jerusalem, according to Hebrews 11:8–16; 12:18–29; and Revelation 21:1–4?

3. The apostle John's book of Revelation is apocalyptic literature, like the visions of Zechariah. As we continue reading Zechariah, it will be good to keep putting his words alongside John's, which unfold even more truth in light of the finished work of Jesus. For example, how does Revelation 21:5–27 similarly point ahead to the completion of Zechariah's prophecies—but with Jesus as the explicit focus?

4. It is important to remember that God's completed people will include both Jews and Gentiles who worship Jesus as Lord. The apostle Paul affirms certain promises for ethnic Jews; we may not fully understand the nature of their fulfillment, but how might you generally summarize the promises given in Romans 11:25–32? How should these promises lead Gentile believers now to pray and act?

DAY FIVE—REVIEW AND REFLECT

1. How must the words of Zechariah 1 have sounded to the original hearers as they struggled to rebuild the temple in the capital city of their kingdom (which was no longer a kingdom)? In what similar ways do these words sound in our ears as believers today?

2. Zechariah 1 is full of the Lord's plans for his chosen people—and also for all the nations of the earth. Referring to specific parts of the chapter, note what aspects of God's sovereign hand over the nations especially instruct and comfort you, in relation to our world today?

3. The ringing command of the book comes in Zechariah 1:3: *"Therefore say to them, Thus declares the Lord of hosts: Return to me, says the Lord of hosts, and I will return to you, says the Lord of hosts."* We've seen how this call came to God's remnant of returned exiles. How does this call speak into your life and into the church today? In what specific ways can you respond even this week?

4. James 4:8–10 and Titus 2:11–14 describe the Christian's life of constant turning and returning to the Lord who saves us through his Son. Conclude by reading and meditating on these verses, praying that we believers will take God's Word to heart as we press on in all our building and rebuilding, looking for the return of our glorious King.

Notes for Lesson 3

Lesson 4 (Zech. 2:1–3:10)

GOD WITH US, THE PURIFIER

We're continuing to hear the word of the Lord from the prophet Zechariah, *urging God's people to return to the Lord and to look in faith for the glorious plan of salvation to be accomplished through the coming King, who would restore Jerusalem in a greater way than they could imagine.* Two visions so far (the heavenly horseman, and the horns and the craftsmen) have brought comfort to the Jewish remnant in the midst of rebuilding their conquered land, especially the temple in Jerusalem. The Lord is showing them that he will have mercy on them, and that he will cast down their enemies.

In this lesson, we'll see the next two visions bringing continued comfort—the third vision focusing on God's blessing of his people with his powerful presence, and the fourth focusing on his cleansing of iniquity from them (illustrated in Joshua the high priest). Through these deepening visions, God's people develop sharper spiritual vision for the unfolding story of redemption that culminates in the promised King Jesus. These prophecies do not name him explicitly, but they point to him more and more clearly as the source of ultimate comfort and cleansing for all the people God will call together to worship him in holiness and glory forever.

As we read these visions, let's marvel as we take them in. They capture our imaginations with their vivid beauty; they show us the salvation planned long ago by our sovereign God; and they draw our hearts to grasp the purifying power of this salvation given to us, his people, through his Son.

DAY ONE—GLORY IN HER MIDST (ZECH. 2:1–13)

1. Read Zechariah 2:1–13. Then give titles and short summations for the following suggested sections:

   a. Zechariah 2:1–5

   b. Zechariah 2:6–9

   c. Zechariah 2:10–12

   d. Zechariah 2:13

2. A measuring line would be used in building and rebuilding—a hopeful indication for a city being restored to
   life (see also Zech. 1:16). But why will a measuring line
   not work for the restored Jerusalem in the first section
   (2:1–5)? What does the climactic revelation God gives
   his people in verse 5 make you see and understand? (See
   also Ex. 40:34–38; 1 Kings 8:10–11.)

3. The third section of this vision (Zech. 2:10–12) provides
   a bookend of comfort, developing the same theme as
   the first. What are the reasons here that God's people
   (called "daughter of Zion") should sing and rejoice?
   What is emphasized in these words from the Lord given
   by Zechariah to a weak and broken-down city of people?
   *Note: The one who speaks of being sent by the Lord (vv. 8, 9, 11)
   appears to be the angel who talks with Zechariah (v. 3), likely the same
   angel of the Lord who began speaking in the first vision (1:7–17).*

4. If we are Gentiles who have come to God through faith in his Son, we are part of the "many nations" in this vision who "join themselves to the LORD" and become his people (Zech. 2:11). The city without walls is growing still! We are called to believe—and yet how do verses 10–12 show the sovereign Lord to be the one who owns and directs the whole process? (Recall Zech. 1:17.)

5. Let's go back to the middle section of this vision (Zech. 2:6–9), which calls the Jews remaining in the northern lands of exile to return to their own land. How would you sum up what God appears to be *after* here, for his people? What phrases from this section remind you of other passages we have seen so far in Haggai and Zechariah?

DAY TWO—BE SILENT AND LOOK; HE'S COMING!

1. In light of what God has said he will do for his people and against his people's oppressors, meditate on the response called for in Zechariah 2:13. For whom is this command, and why?

2. As we quiet ourselves to respond and to look for the Lord's "rousing himself" to come dwell with us, we peer through layers of time to view his coming. As we've seen, these visions first encourage the remnant in their rebuilding of Jerusalem, but they also reach ahead in the redemptive story. Think of God's promises to dwell and to "be the glory" in the people's midst (Zech. 2:5, 10, 11). Then summarize how Christ's incarnation fulfilled those promises in a way the Old Testament Jews only glimpsed. (See, for example, Matt. 1:22–23; John 1:14.)

3. How does the gift of the indwelling Holy Spirit to believers today offer another layer of fulfillment to this promise of God's presence among his people? (See, for example, John 14:25–26; Acts 2:1–21.)

4. We've already looked ahead to the final layer of fulfillment shown in the heavenly Jerusalem promised to all God's people. We can't look there often enough—and the apocalyptic visions of Zechariah point us there repeatedly. Read Hebrews 12:18–29 one more time; how do these verses make the promise of Zechariah 2:5 even more awesome?

5. Look again to Revelation 21:1–27—the Bible's culminating picture of this heavenly city. As in Zechariah, we see here an instrument for measuring the city: it is a perfect cube, measuring "foursquare" (Rev. 21:16). In this way, it is like "the Most Holy Place" in the temple, where the ark of the covenant signified God's presence (1 Kings 6:16; see also vv. 19–20). In John's vision there *are* city walls, described in dazzling detail. What various truths does the vision of Revelation 21 emphasize, while affirming the consistent focus on God dwelling with his people?

DAY THREE—GOD GIVES CLEAN CLOTHES
(ZECH. 3:1–5)

1. Zechariah 2 ends with the Lord inheriting Judah "as his portion in the holy land" (v. 12) and rousing himself from his "holy dwelling" (v. 13). How can this holy God dwell with his sinful people? This is the question addressed in the fourth vision. Read through Zechariah 3, and assign titles and short summations for the following two sections:

a. Zechariah 3:1–5

b. Zechariah 3:6–10

2. Picture the courtroom-like scene (Zech. 3:1). Recall that Joshua the high priest and Zerubbabel the governor together led the remnant in the temple-rebuilding project (see also Hag. 1:1). The high priest was the one to enter the Most Holy Place each year on the Day of Atonement, to offer sacrifices for his sins and the sins of the people. In this vision, as in reality, he represented God's people in God's holy presence. Here again we meet the angel of the Lord, who responds to Satan's accusations of Joshua with a repeated rebuke. According to verse 2, what are the grounds for the Lord's rebuke, and why are Satan's accusations futile?

3. And yet Satan addresses a problem: the high priest is clothed with filthy garments—which clearly represent iniquity, or sin. In Zechariah 3:3–5, what is the role of Joshua in dealing with his dirty clothes? What is the role of the angel of the Lord? What do we learn here?

4. Stop to consider the Bible's consistent message that, ever since Adam and Eve sinned, we fallen human beings are like ones dressed in filthy rags before a holy God. Read the following, jotting down phrases that stand out: Isaiah 64:6; Romans 3:10–12. How had God's people seen this truth in their own history?

5. But let us be quick to consider God's mercy in forgiving his people's sin—removing their filthy clothes and giving them clean clothes to wear. As this remnant of God's people followed God's provision in the ceremonial law, offering their sacrifices before him, they were trusting God's word. They were believing God's promises. Through faith they could rejoice in God's forgiveness and salvation. How might Zechariah's first audience have connected his fourth vision with Psalm 32:1–5, Psalm 51:1–2, and Isaiah 61:10? Choose one of these references to comment on.

DAY FOUR—GOD'S SERVANT THE BRANCH
(ZECH. 3:6–10)

1. Joshua the high priest in pure vestments seems now to provide a transition to the sinless High Priest to come. What amazing blessings does the angel tell him will be his if he walks in God's ways (Zech. 3:6–7)? Look ahead to the greater, perfect High Priest, Jesus Christ: What blessings did he bring, through what kind of sacrifice, according to Hebrews 9:11–14?

2. In the conclusion of this vision, Zechariah prophesies the coming of the One who will accomplish this cleansing from sin once and for all. From the stump of the cut-down kingdom will come a lowly "Branch" that will grow and bear amazing fruit. Look for the "servant" and the "Branch" in Isaiah 11:1–5; 42:1–9; Jeremiah 23:5–6; 33:14–16. Sum up the way in which these verses help explain the great announcement of Zechariah 3:8.

3. The engraved stone with seven eyes (Zech. 3:9) is not so clear; it might relate to the high priest's ephod and breastpiece inset with precious stones that represented the tribes of Israel and were engraved with their names (Ex. 28:6–21). It might picture the stone of the rebuilt temple. The most striking statement, though, comes at the end of Zechariah 3:9. What will God do, and why is this statement so amazing?

4. Zechariah 3:10 echoes a description of great King Solomon's peaceful, fruitful kingdom (compare 1 Kings 4:25). How does this description point us to what King Jesus accomplished for his people, now his church (compare Eph. 2:11–22)?

5. How does Revelation 19:6–8 complete the Bible's picture of God's redeemed people dressed in new, clean clothes?

DAY FIVE—REVIEW AND REFLECT

1. In what specific ways have these visions in Zechariah 2–3 deepened the book's call to God's people to return to the Lord and to look in faith for the glorious plan of salvation to be accomplished through the coming King, who would restore Jerusalem in a greater way than they could imagine?

2. The promises of Zechariah 2 affirm God's hand in rebuilding and protecting Jerusalem; the struggling remnant could trust the God who faithfully watches over his people. How would you as a citizen of the "spiritual Jerusalem" sum up your own thanksgiving for these promises? How can these promises encourage and strengthen the church today?

3. In what ways do you identify personally with the vision of Joshua the high priest in filthy garments—and then pure, clean ones? Look back through Zechariah 3 and write down several truths about God's salvation that instruct and strengthen you.

4. Read 1 Peter 2:4–10. We need no high priest other than Christ—and, trusting in him, we believers become a community of priests, with access to God and offering acceptable sacrifices to him, through Christ our Lord. What are our central goals as this spiritual house, this holy priesthood?

5. How might Zechariah 2–3 affect your prayers even this day or this week? What thanksgivings will you offer? What petitions will you bring for yourself, or for a friend who struggles with sin or guilt, or for the church both near you and around the world?

Notes for Lesson 4

Lesson 5 (Zech. 4:1–6:15)

GOD REVEALS
HIS REDEMPTIVE PLANS

Zechariah 1–3 presented the first four visions, culminating in the figure of Joshua the high priest—and pointing forward finally to the "Branch" to come. This lesson covers the remaining five visions (the final one calling for a symbolic action), which unfold similar themes of God's plan for a restored temple, his presence with his people, his dealing with their sin, and his lordship over the nations of the earth.

The visions have a symmetry to them: the patrolling horsemen at the start of the first four visions are matched by patrolling horses and chariots at the end of the second four, and this second grouping also culminates in the figure of Joshua—pointing forward also to the Branch to come. Zerubbabel's leadership is again affirmed in this second group of visions; the two leaders, Zerubbabel and Joshua, continue to be key to God's work among his returned exiles at this stage of rebuilding Jerusalem.

These visions are strange and stranger to us as we read—as they would have been also to God's people in 520 BC. What a grace that God breaks into the ordinary drudgery of little things, as we set one stone upon another, with pictures that capture our imaginations and pull our thoughts to heavenly things! They pull our thoughts ultimately toward the heavenly King, the Branch, the great High Priest, our Lord and Savior Jesus Christ, and his glorious plan of salvation that will finally restore Jerusalem in a greater way than any of us can imagine.

As you wash your dishes this week, drive your car, discipline those children, write that report, encourage that friend, may your heart be encouraged by the grand gospel story of which you are a part. "The Lord of the whole earth" (Zech. 4:14) watches over you and every one of his beloved people, to the end.

DAY ONE—BY MY SPIRIT, SAYS THE LORD (ZECH. 4:1–7)

1. After the climactic vision of Joshua the high priest, the visions resume, with the same "angel who talked with me" (Zech. 4:1) rousing Zechariah again to see more of these visions, which appear to take place in one night. Read Zechariah 4:1–3 and write a few initial observations and questions.

2. Draw a simple picture or write a brief description of the picture given here, as clearly as you can see it!

3. Stop to consider the nature and tone of the dialogue between the prophet and the angel in Zechariah 4:1–5. What human and heavenly qualities are variously in view? How do you respond?

4. Before giving any specific interpretation of this shining lampstand with seven lamps flowing with oil, the angel delivers the spiritual meaning. The central statement comes in Zechariah 4:6 (see also Hag. 2:5). What is the great truth here, and why did Zerubbabel in particular so need to hear it? Why do you?

5. Zechariah 4:7 promises the Lord's completion of what he has decreed—no matter what mountain (what obstacle) seems to stand in the way. The "top stone" (the capstone completing the building) will be put in place by the leader chosen by God to do it. Then what will the people shout, and why? What are we learning here about the way in which God accomplishes his plan for human history?

Day Two—The Day of Small Things
(Zech. 4:8–14)

1. Zechariah 4:8–10a continues the encouragement of God's promise that the temple rebuilding will be completed under the leadership of Zerubbabel, the same man who began it. What will be the lessons learned when this outcome finally comes to pass?

2. Take some time to meditate on Zechariah 4:10a. Remind yourself of the ways in which the people in Zechariah's context were tempted to despise "the day of small things." How are you sometimes likewise tempted, as you do the ordinary daily work God has put before you?

3. This vision concludes with more specific questions and answers concerning the significance of symbolic details. In Zechariah 4:10b the angel points toward the meaning of the seven things glimpsed earlier as seven eyes in 3:9 and perhaps again as seven lamps in 4:2. (The number seven often symbolizes perfection or completion.) How does the angel's interpretation of "these seven" confirm and deepen the point of this vision (and all these visions)?

4. The angel seems to think Zechariah should know the identity of the olive trees with the two branches filling the lampstand full of golden oil (Zech. 4:11–14). Readers guess that these two "anointed ones" picture either Zerubbabel and Joshua (representing Israel's kingly and priestly offices), or perhaps Zechariah and Haggai. In any case, we see a picture of God's Spirit filling his chosen leaders with life and strength to lead—so that his people become like a brilliant lampstand, shining God's very presence throughout the earth. How do Isaiah 62:1 and Revelation 1:20 shed light on Zechariah's vision?

5. But we must see the One who "holds the seven stars in his right hand, who walks among the seven golden lampstands" (Rev. 2:1). That is Jesus Christ, "the light of the world" (John 8:12), the one who sent the Holy Spirit to dwell in his church after he rose from the dead and ascended into heaven (John 14:16–17). Now, reread Zechariah 4:1–14. What does this vision cause you to pray, as you pray in the name of the Lord Jesus Christ?

DAY THREE—LIFT YOUR EYES TO SEE (ZECH. 5:1–11)

1. In the sixth vision (Zech. 5:1–4), the prophet sees a huge flying scroll that is inscribed on both sides, as were the tablets of the Ten Commandments (Ex. 32:15). Although the sins of stealing and lying are named specifically, how does this picture seem to address sinfulness in general, on a larger scale?

2. What is frightening about this vision in Zechariah 5:1–4? But how does this vision give hope? (Refer to specific details in the text.)

3. By the seventh vision, it seems Zechariah may be getting tired. Or perhaps he is downcast by the pervasive sin exposed in the previous vision. But he is not done. What does the angel call him to lift his eyes and see, and what details help explain the nature of it (Zech. 5:5–8)?

4. Two women are carrying this basket of iniquity far away, to Babylon (which often represents a place of evil, where God's enemies dwell). What parts of this vision in Zechariah 5:9–11 strike you and encourage you?

5. God's people had a history of repeated sinfulness, as we have seen. They may have wondered if they would ever be free from their sin. What great truth do both visions in Zechariah 5 reveal to them and to us? Before answering, read Psalm 103:6–14.

DAY FOUR—CHARIOTS AND A CROWN
(ZECH. 6:1–15)

1. The eighth vision recalls the first; read Zechariah 6:1–8, and look back to Zechariah 1:7–17, to find the similar impression and thrust of the visions. What are we vividly seeing about our God here, in relation to the whole wide world and all its activity? What details stand out and why?

2. Again recall the historical context, with this little returned remnant that is subject to the Persian Empire and surrounded by unfriendly peoples, but still called to rebuild the temple in Jerusalem. Why would these far-reaching visions be especially encouraging to these Israelites?

3. The final picture (Zech. 6:9–15) is one to be *acted out* by Zechariah: he is to make a crown from silver and gold taken from a group of exiles arrived from Babylonia, and to crown Joshua the high priest. Throughout Israel's history, the lines of kingship and of priesthood had always been separate—but in this symbolic portrayal they merge.

   a. To whom does the crowned figure point, according to Zechariah 6:12–14? (See Lesson Four, Day Four, and recall Zech. 3:7–8.) What things do we know about this figure?

b. Another Old Testament priest-king appeared early on to Abraham (see Gen. 14:17–20). According to Hebrews 7:1–3, in what ways does this figure resemble Christ?

c. Briefly summarize how the Lord Jesus provides the full meaning of these foreshadowings. (See Heb. 7:11–17; 7:23–8:2.)

4. In Zechariah 6:15, what kinds of responses to God's Word are portrayed on the part of God's people? What details in this verse show the great mercy of God's Word to us, as he reveals his redemptive plan? What does this verse lead you to pray?

DAY FIVE—REVIEW AND REFLECT

1. We've done five visions in one lesson . . . perhaps not as taxing as Zechariah's one night full of all these visions! Look back through the visions in Zechariah 4:1–6:15, and write a few summary reflections on how they bring into even clearer focus Zechariah's call to God's people *to return to the Lord and to look in faith for the glorious plan of salvation to be accomplished through the coming King, who would restore Jerusalem in a greater way than they could imagine.*

2. These chapters emphasize *eyes* and *seeing*; Zechariah himself must repeatedly *lift his eyes* to see. How might the angel's call to "lift your eyes and see" (5:5) speak to you, and to the church today?

3. Referring to specific passages or verses from this week's
   Scripture text, make a list of the qualities of God we can
   discern as we receive this amazing revelation from him.
   Looking through what you have written, spend some
   time in praise and worship of the Lord God.

4. Zechariah brings God's Word for God's people to receive
   together; we receive this Word today in the full light of
   King Jesus, who came, who died, who rose again, and
   who is head of the church redeemed by his blood. In
   what ways have these visions encouraged you to think,
   pray, and live not just individually but as a part of the
   people of God?

Notes for Lesson 5

Lesson 6 (Zech. 7:1–8:23)

GOD SPEAKS TRUTH
AND PEACE

After the nighttime visions given by God in chapters 1–6, these middle two chapters wake us up with a bit more direct preaching. The ninth month of the fourth year of King Darius (Zech. 7:1) is two years after the earlier prophecies (see 1:1), and about two years before the temple rebuilding would be completed. In the midst of the rebuilding, God is reminding his people what true worship and faith in him are all about: not empty ritual but rather hearts and lives full of devotion to God, kindness and mercy to one another, and blessing overflowing in God's presence.

These two chapters tell bad news and good news. Zechariah 7 exposes the falsely religious among God's people, revealing their hard hearts and showing the consequences of their sin: a desolate Jerusalem. But chapter 8 reveals God's faithful saving love for his people, as he calls them to lives of obedience and blessing—in a Jerusalem full of peace and filled with followers from many nations.

As we hear God's strong words to his people released from exile and rebuilding the Jerusalem temple, we again see how this book of Zechariah points far ahead, to the coming of the promised King and to a heavenly Jerusalem that will never be destroyed. As they wait for their King, God calls his people to return to him and to live in faith and true worship, according to his word. God's call comes to the church today, both convicting us of our sin and comforting us with eternal hope, through Christ our Lord.

Day One—God Answers a Question
(Zech. 7:1–7)

1. In Zechariah 7:1–3, a contingent from Bethel (just north of Jerusalem) comes to Jerusalem, asking the priests and prophets whether the people should continue certain days of fasting established during the exile. The Old Testament law included just one fast, the Day of Atonement (Lev. 23:27). But the exiled Jews had established four different fasts commemorating the attack and fall of Jerusalem and the temple; now that the rebuilding was progressing well, couldn't those extra fasts be discontinued? Read and then summarize the response from God in verses 4–6.

2. Read Zechariah 7:7, which refers to prophets in pre-
   exilic days, before Judah with its capital, Jerusalem, fell.
   Isaiah was one of those prophets. In what ways does the
   message in Isaiah 58:1–5 resonate with the one we're
   hearing in Zechariah? What does this continuity show
   about God—and about sinful human beings?

3. Consider again Zechariah 7:5–6. In what ways might we
   in the church today be like those who fast (or perform
   various acts of worship) *for ourselves*, as opposed to doing
   it *for the Lord*?

4. How might the following verses help us explain the difference? See Matthew 6:16–18, Luke 18:9–14, and John
   5:39–44 (spoken by Jesus to Jews who rejected him).

DAY TWO—LEARNING FROM THE PAST
(ZECH. 7:8–14)

1. True worshipers of the Lord will hear and obey his Word: their faith will *show*, especially in the way they care for one another and for those around them. Read the Lord's call in Zechariah 7:8–10; how are these commands organized, and what seems to be the emphasis? (Similar themes appear throughout the prophets—for example, in Isaiah 1:16–17, Jeremiah 22:3, and Micah 6:8.)

2. Zechariah 7:11–12a describes how those who received this call from the former prophets responded. What words and phrases in these verses help reveal the awfulness of their response?

3. The next words describe the Lord's response to his people's sinful rebellion (Zech. 7:12b–14). List the various components of the Lord's response. What can we observe here about the nature of God and the nature of sin?

4. Look back through Zechariah 7 to find its strong emphasis on the word of the Lord. What truths about God's Word stand out? What might this chapter make us pray concerning God's Word (and concerning our hearts)?

DAY THREE—WHAT THE LORD SAYS HE WILL DO
(ZECH. 8:1–19)

1. To begin, read through Zechariah 8, noting each use of the name "the LORD of hosts." What is the thrust of this chapter, and how is the identity of "the LORD of hosts" centrally important?

2. Zechariah 7 ended with the land desolate. Chapter 8 portrays its full restoration, centered in Jerusalem (also called Zion), the place God chose to show his dwelling with his people. First, review Zechariah 1:3, 14–17; 2:10–12. Then read Zechariah 8:1–8. Where is God in this picture? Where are his people? What details stand out, and why?

3. God says clearly what he will do: "*I will save*" (Zech. 8:7, 13). However, through God's strength his people are called to act as well: What repeated commands come in verses 9, 13, and 15? As they obey, what kinds of peace and security does God promise his people in verses 9–15?

4. Zechariah 8:16–19 calls for further response—and offers more promises!

   a. What repeated words do you find in these verses, and why are these words so crucial for God's true gathering of worshipers? How can we tell God is calling here not just for good actions but also for pure hearts?

b. According to verse 19, the four fasts commemorating Jerusalem's fall will turn into *what*? So, then, how does God ultimately answer the question of the contingent from Bethel (7:1–3)?

5. Think back to the visions of Zechariah 1–6, especially those concerning God's purifying his people from sin. How does the preaching of chapters 7–8 build on the visions of the preceding chapters?

DAY FOUR—EVEN A BIGGER PROMISE (ZECH. 8:20–23)

1. In Zechariah 8:20–23, there is a lot of motion! Note the various terms that describe who is in motion and why. What is being pictured here?

2. Recall Genesis 12:1–3 and Isaiah 2:2–3; 66:18–21. Write down a few phrases from these passages that show what God's plan has been from the beginning, regarding the nations of the world.

3. When will we see this streaming of all the nations to the presence of the Lord? Consider the ways in which we are seeing it right now, as people from all over the world are hearing and believing the gospel of Jesus Christ. Jesus the Son of God brought God's very presence to us in the flesh: he is our spiritual temple, and we today are among the seekers drawn to a heavenly Jerusalem through Jesus who died to save us. Turn again to John 2:13–22 and Hebrews 12:22–24; how do these passages help to point to the fulfillment of Zechariah 8:20–23?

4. These promises of God applied to the postexilic Jews rebuilding Jerusalem, and they reach out to the climactic first coming of Jesus—and beyond. We've turned to the book of Revelation multiple times, and we have to keep turning there! Look back through Zechariah 8, and find wonderful connections in Revelation 7:9–12; 21:1–3.

DAY FIVE—REVIEW AND REFLECT

1. The book of Zechariah *urges God's people to return to the Lord and to look in faith for the glorious plan of salvation to be accomplished through the coming King, who would restore Jerusalem in a greater way than they could imagine.* What parts of this overall theme are especially deepened in Zechariah 7–8? Briefly explain your answer.

2. These two chapters look back to learn from the past before looking ahead to the future. What are some of the ways we can apply this principle to us believers today?

3. Colossians 1:3–8 reveals how the gospel was practiced and growing among the believers in Colossae. In light of the challenges to God's people in Zechariah 7–8, what similar important themes does the apostle Paul put before the Colossian Christians—and before us as the body of Christ today? In what ways does God's Word pierce your heart to pray concerning your "love . . . for all the saints" (Col. 1:4)?

4. To close, read and pray Psalm 67. How does this psalm capture the thrust of Zechariah 7–8? May God's Word stretch our hearts to pray prayers as big as his promises!

Notes for Lesson 6

Lesson 7 (Zech. 9:1–11:17)

God Declares
Salvation and Judgment

Zechariah 9 begins the final section of the book, following the visions of chapters 1–6 and the encouragement/challenge of chapters 7–8. The book's first two sections addressed the people in the midst of rebuilding the temple; the final section comes later, at an undefined time, and with a different tone—even more grandly prophetic and far-reaching.

Looking at the text, we see immediately that Zechariah 9 begins a section of poetry, which we see in our translations as parallel lines. These lines reflect the balancing units of meaning (most often two parallel units, sometimes more) through which Hebrew poetry delivers its message. The poetry is exceptionally condensed, full of imagery, and able to pierce the thoughts and imaginations of our hearts with dramatic impact. What a gift—the powerful, Spirit-breathed language through which the Lord ordained his Word to come to us. Let's take note of the poetry and how it works, as we read it.

As the capstone of his prophecy, the writer Zechariah delivers two "burdens," or "oracles" (beginning in Zech. 9:1 and 12:1), words of brilliant promise for followers of Yahweh but devastating judgment for those who reject him. As we will see, these ending burdens deepen and in fact complete the book's *call to God's people to return to the Lord and to look in faith for the glorious plan of salvation to be accomplished through the coming King, who would restore Jerusalem in a greater way than they could imagine.* The King's person and work become even more clear and vivid in these final chapters. The final Old Testament prophets are pointing us straight ahead to King Jesus.

DAY ONE—GOD'S EYE ON MANKIND (ZECH. 9:1–8)

1. Zechariah 8 ended with a prophecy of many peoples outside of Judah being drawn to seek the Lord. Chapter 9 begins with a contrast, showing many cities and nations that remain enemies of the Lord and his people. From what perspective are these peoples presented in verses 1–8? How can we tell? (Note especially the matching pictures in vv. 1 and 8.)

2. Recall the prophecy of Zechariah 1:20–21, concerning those who "lifted up their horns against the land of Judah." Zechariah 9:1–7 names some of them. In the places listed here, many find a prophecy of Persian strongholds that would in 333 BC be invaded and conquered from north to south in this order by Alexander the Great, ushering in a period of Greek supremacy. In what ways is the nature of the sin in these places described, and how do the declared punishments answer the sin?

3. Interestingly, in Alexander the Great's rampage of this region, Jerusalem was not touched. Whether or not this prophecy is that specific, what truths do we learn about the Lord and his care for his people in Zechariah 9:8?

4. Think about the current unrest and injustice in the world. Then think back to the horsemen in Zechariah 1:8–11, along with the picture of God's all-seeing eye in Zechariah 9. Then read through Psalm 94:1–11. How do you respond?

Day Two—The Coming King (Zech. 9:9–17)

1. We often hear Zechariah 9:9 quoted on Palm Sunday; how wonderful to read it in context! Review Zechariah 6:11–13, and then read 9:9–10 to see this promised King even more vividly. Write a list of observations from verses 9–10 about this King. What details stand out? *Note: Ephraim in the north and Jerusalem in the south refer to both halves of the kingdom of Israel.*

2. We don't have to wonder how this prophecy was fulfilled. Read Matthew 21:1–5, Luke 19:35–38, and John 12:12–16. How do the Gospels show the fulfillment of Zechariah 9:9–10?

3. Old Testament prophecies are often described as mountain ranges glimpsed in layers stretching out in the distance. We suggested that Zechariah 9:1–8 might point ahead to Alexander the Great's battle march of 333 BC. Verse 13 affirms this specific focus, mentioning future victorious battles of the Jews against Greece—which in fact occurred in the Maccabean revolt of 166–160 BC. In verses 11–15, in what ways are we shown that in these battles it is the Lord himself who fights for his people?

4. We've seen that this whole section reaches far into the future—to Christ and his kingly rule. Zechariah 9:16–17 seems again to peer not just to coming battles with Greeks but also farther ahead. According to these verses, what is God's central work for his people, and what various pictures show the beauty of his perfect care for them? Where *do* we, and where *will* we, see this beauty of the Lord's saved people shining forth? *Note: The phrase "on that day" often points ahead to momentous events of salvation and judgment. We saw this phrase in Haggai 2:23. We will see this phrase again.*

DAY THREE—GOD THE JUDGE AND THE REDEEMER
(ZECH. 10:1–11:3)

1. In Zechariah 10:1–2, what contrasts emerge between seeking the true Lord God and seeking false gods?

2. The Lord holds responsible his people's leaders (probably including unfaithful priests, false prophets, heads of families): they are not shepherding "the flock of his people" (Zech. 9:16) but have let the sheep "wander" (Zech. 10:2). Zechariah must have witnessed some of these shepherds taking control—and we know that by New Testament times, there were many of them. In Zechariah 10:3 and 11:1–3, what dramatic words and pictures show God's judgment on these bad shepherds? What do you see, and what do you hear?

3. Sandwiched between words of judgment are glorious promises of deliverance from the Lord, the one true Shepherd. Read Zechariah 10:3c–12, first just to take in this marvelous prophecy of the Lord's gathering all his redeemed people in a kind of second exodus—but this time from many nations.

   a. How must this prophecy have comforted the remnant of faithful Jews in their weakened and fragmented state?

   b. How does this prophecy comfort and instruct us in the church today? Consider the following verses, or others that come to mind, and write down some ways Zechariah's words point us to the One who came to accomplish the redemption of his people from all the nations: Matthew 9:36; John 10:1–18.

4. Look back through Zechariah 10. What sorts of prayers might this chapter encourage us to pray? Speak and/or write a few specific prayers in response to this part of God's Word.

DAY FOUR—FOOLISH SHEPHERD, DOOMED SHEEP (ZECH. 11:1–17)

1. This "burden" ends with words of heavy judgment on the people of Israel who do not follow God, both shepherds and sheep. Zechariah 11:1–3 refers back to 10:3, as we have seen, but it also frames this chapter along with verse 17. Read Zechariah 11:1–17 and write your initial observations. What seems to be the main idea?

2. In Zechariah 11, the Lord commands Zechariah to act out this final judgment: he is first to become shepherd of a "flock doomed to slaughter" (vv. 4, 7). Many of the details are hard to interpret—such as the "three shepherds" (v. 8), possibly three unfaithful leaders in Zechariah's time. Zechariah's two staffs help make the point: What do their names signify, and what is shown by their breaking (vv. 7–14)?

3. The thirty pieces of silver catch our attention—and bring to mind the one among Jesus's chosen leaders who betrayed him. Read Matthew 27:3–10, which alludes both to Zechariah 11:12–13 and to Jeremiah 19:1–13. (Matthew references only Jeremiah, the more prominent prophet.) How does the story of Judas shed light on Zechariah's prophecy?

4. First, then, Zechariah takes the role of a good shepherd rejected by wandering sheep—who are finally rejected by him. But then in Zechariah 11:15–17 he plays the role of a bad shepherd, representing evil leaders who ultimately destroy the people they are called to protect. Read through Matthew 23:1–39. How do Jesus's words here resonate with Zechariah's? (Find specific references!) And how does Jesus himself show us that he is the one true Good Shepherd?

Day Five—Review and Reflect

1. This first "burden of the word of the Lord" has been full of warnings, giving sober weight to Zechariah's call to God's people to return to the Lord (Zech. 1:3). In what ways might Zechariah 9–11 call you to self-examination, repentance, and ever more faithful returning to the Lord? Refer to specific verses in your answer.

2. This burden has also been lit up with promises of salvation—shining more brilliantly in the darkness of sin and
   judgment. Look back through Zechariah 9–11 again, and
   summarize what we have glimpsed about the one we
   see coming to save his people? How does this summary
   strengthen and encourage you today?

3. In what specific ways might Zechariah 9–11 encourage
   us to pray for our leaders in the church? Consider also
   1 Peter 5:1–5 and Acts 20:26–35 (from Paul's last words
   to the Ephesian elders).

4. Let's end this lesson looking again at Jesus. *How* are we
   to respond to him, according to Zechariah 9:9? Spend
   some moments rejoicing before the Lord, thanking him
   that he sent his Son, "righteous and having salvation"
   for sinners like us. *"For our sake he [God] made him to be sin
   who knew no sin, so that in him we might become the righteousness
   of God"* (2 Cor. 5:21).

Notes for Lesson 7

Lesson 8
(Zech. 12:1–14:21)

GOD OUR KING WILL COME

We come to the final chapters of Zechariah's prophecy. Its far-reaching vision grows and grows to the end.

Let's remember where we've come so far, in this grand book that calls God's people *to return to the Lord and to look in faith for the glorious plan of salvation to be accomplished through the coming King, who would restore Jerusalem in a greater way than they could imagine.* First, Zechariah 1–6 presented nine visual revelations from the Lord given in the midst of temple rebuilding—symbolic pictures of the restoration ordained by God for Jerusalem and of the one through whom he would accomplish it. In Zechariah 7–8 (two years later, with the people still rebuilding) came a message from the Lord reminding them what true worship and faith in him are all about: *not* empty ritual but hearts and lives full of devotion to God, kindness and mercy to one another, and blessing overflowing in his presence.

Zechariah 9 introduced the two "burdens," later oracles that reach out in time: the first (Zech. 9–11) focused on God's saving of his true flock and his destruction of enemies without and bad shepherds within. Now the second burden (Zech. 12–14) looks ahead to a siege of nations against God's people, from which God will bring them victorious, strong, and holy—with a King who reigns over all the earth.

The details of Zechariah 12–14 are notoriously difficult to understand. The promises, however, are magnificent and important for us as God's people to hear and heed, especially as they point so clearly to the Lord Jesus. Our goal will be not to pin them all down to a specific time frame but to plant them in our minds and hearts so that the Holy Spirit might use them to shape our thoughts and prayers as we live through our part of the last days.

DAY ONE—ON THAT DAY (ZECH. 12:1–9)

1. In Zechariah 12:1, what does the Lord want us to remember about him? As you look through verses 1–9, how does the perspective of verse 1 make a difference? As you live your life tomorrow, how can the perspective of verse 1 make a difference?

2. In Zechariah 12:1-9, what frightening experience is prophesied for God's people, but what strong promises are given at the same time? Note the various pictures through which God makes this message vivid.

3. But when does this siege of Jerusalem occur? In Zechariah 12:1–9, find the repeating phrase "on that day," a phrase similar to "the day of the Lord," that often points ahead to momentous events of salvation and judgment.

   a. Look back to "that day" in Zechariah 9:16 and Haggai 2:20–23. How do both passages in their contexts seem to point ahead to various layers of future events both nearer and farther away?

b. How does the New Testament light up the meaning of "that day"? Summarize what you find in 1 Thessalonians 4:16–5:4; 2 Thessalonians 1:7–10; 2 Peter 3:10–12.

4. Until that day, God's people know what it means to be *besieged*. What examples can you think of, past and present? As we read of worldwide war in Revelation 16:14–16; 17:14; 19:11–16, what truths can we affirm with soberness and yet shining hope?

5. How does Zechariah 12:1–9 let us glimpse the Lord's sovereign hand over human history from the beginning to the end? In what ways does this view of human history differ from many of the views around us today?

DAY TWO—THE ONE THEY HAVE PIERCED (ZECH. 12:10–13:1)

1. From Zechariah 12:10–13:1, write down everything you can observe happening in the house of David and the inhabitants of Jerusalem "on that day." What details stand out? *Note: Verse 11 probably refers to the great mourning that had followed the death of good King Josiah (2 Chron. 35:24).*

2. Although we cannot always discern the exact timing of these prophecies, we can discern their pointing to Jesus. How does John 19:31–37 in the New Testament guide our interpretation of Zechariah 12:10–13:1?

3. This prophecy of Zechariah seems to grow in application the more we ponder it. How might the mourning, the grace, and the pleas for mercy apply to every sinner drawn to contemplate in faith the death of Jesus, who bore our sin in our place on the cross? How does this prophecy reach ahead to Christ's second coming, according to Revelation 1:5–7?

4. Think back through Zechariah: How has he consistently shown our great need for God's merciful cleansing from sin? Along with Zechariah 12:10–13:1, consider passages such as Zechariah 3:1–10 and 5:5–11.

5. Meditate on that picture of the fountain in Zechariah 13:1. What is so wonderful about that picture?

DAY THREE—GOD WILL CLEANSE HIS LAND (ZECH. 13:2–9)

1. In Zechariah 13:2–6, in what ways do we see the effects of that cleansing fountain in verse 1? Why are the evils removed here such significant ones for God's chosen people?

2. Zechariah 13:7 is an awesome verse, in which the Lord God refers to "the man who stands next to me," one whom God calls "my shepherd"—the Good Shepherd, not the worthless one. God calls for the sword to strike him. In Matthew 26:26–32, how does the Good Shepherd himself show us where this verse is pointing?

3. In what ways do we see God the Father and God the Son accomplishing our salvation at the cross? Along with Zechariah 13:7, consider John 10:14–18 and Isaiah 53:6, 10–12.

4. Read Zechariah 13:8–9.

   a. Summarize the process described here, and the result?

b. How might these verses apply to the Jewish people following Jesus's death and resurrection? (Recall again the promises related to ethnic Jews in Romans 11:25–29.)

c. What can we learn from these verses about God's way of refining all those he calls his own, and about his ultimate goal for them? See also 1 Peter 1:1–7.

Day Four—That Day Is Coming
(Zech. 14:1–21)

The final part of Zechariah's final burden is weighty indeed. Read Zechariah 14:1–21, noting the repeated "on that day"; these verses stretch far ahead. We should not expect to pin down every prophecy here in relation to historical events; many seem to relate to the physical city of Jerusalem, for example, but many also seem to reach much farther—to the heavenly Jerusalem we have repeatedly mentioned, that dwelling-with-God promised us in the new heaven and earth (Heb. 12:22–24; Rev. 21). Let's take in these concluding verses deeply and prayerfully, so that we will be ready to receive their fulfillment as God rolls out his plan for human history, culminating in the second coming, the final judgment, and the eternal reign of his glorious Son along with his redeemed people from all the nations of the earth.

1. What are your initial impressions and observations of Zechariah 14? How is this an appropriate conclusion to a book calling God's people to return to him and to look for the coming King?

2. Zechariah 14:1–5 (like Zech. 12:1–9) pictures a battle of all the nations against Jerusalem. What details reveal the horror of the battle (vv. 1–2), and what details reveal the greatness of God's victory against those nations (vv. 3–5)?

3. Zechariah 14:6–11 pictures the rescued and restored city. What details in this passage are echoed in the apostle John's vision of Revelation 21:1–22:5? (See also Rev. 11:15 and 19:15–16.) Take time to dwell on these scenes. What (or *who*) is in the center?

4. Zechariah 14:12–19 vividly shows the great final division between those who worship the King and those who oppose him. Make a list of the various awful ends prophesied for the enemies of God. What should be our response to such painful prophecies? Why are they crucial for us to read? *Note: The Feast of Booths or Tabernacles, celebrated at harvest time just before the rainy season, represents an acknowledgment of God's provision for his people, especially looking back to his care for them in the wilderness after the exodus from Egypt.*

5. The book of Zechariah ends with a picture of complete holiness! Sin is done away with!

   a. Read Zechariah 14:20–21; what details stand out?

   b. In what ways do we know this perfect cleansing now, through the blood of Christ? (See also Heb. 10:1–14.)

c.   But in what ways do we still struggle and long for our sanctification to be complete? How does looking forward to this city spur you on? Can you hear the bells?

DAY FIVE—REVIEW AND REFLECT

1. In what ways does Zechariah 12–14 leave believers with a sober warning concerning living in this sinful world until the final deliverance comes? How well do we teach such warnings to the next generation—and how might we do better?

2. Zechariah has consistently focused not just on God's people but on all the nations of the earth. As you look back through the final chapters (and through the book), what expressions of hope for the nations do you find? In what ways does Zechariah portray the fulfillment of God's promise to Abraham in Genesis 12:3? (And how do you respond?)

3. Zechariah's final chapters are full of motion as they press toward the coming "day of the Lord"! In what ways do you or don't you view your life as heading toward that day? How might these chapters or this book encourage you to look and long for the Lord's appearing?

4. This book calls God's people *to return to the Lord and to look in faith for the glorious plan of salvation to be accomplished through the coming King, who would restore Jerusalem in a greater way than they could imagine.* Zechariah pictures King Jesus in a variety of ways. What are some of the ways you find in the book and especially in these final chapters? How has Zechariah pointed you to Jesus, who died for you, who rose from the dead, who reigns at God's right hand, and who is coming again?

5. Finally, take a moment to write or speak your prayers as you look back through the pages of Zechariah. How might this book call you to repent before a sovereign, holy Lord of hosts who made the heavens and earth and everything in them . . . to trust this sovereign God who directs the course of nations . . . to care more about the nations . . . to pay more attention to the word of the Lord . . . to thank him for our Savior, who was pierced for our transgressions . . . to pursue holiness in eager preparation for that coming day . . . ? What might this book make you pray?

Notes for Lesson 8

Lesson 9 (Mal. 1:1–3:5)

GOD REBUKES HIS PEOPLE
AND DECLARES HIS PLAN

The name *Malachi* means "my messenger." Through this prophet the Lord sends his final message to his people before the four hundred years of waiting that separate the Old and New Testaments. We will see that the messenger Malachi points across these four centuries to another messenger—who will point to the final messenger, the Lord himself, who comes down from heaven.

Malachi looks with clarity not just far ahead but also right around him, condemning the faithless state of the Jewish remnant now resettled in their Persian-ruled territory of Judah. This last Old Testament prophet comes probably about eighty years after Haggai and Zechariah; the temple has been rebuilt, but all those brilliant promises of a great, shining Jerusalem may seem questionable in light of continued servitude, oppressive neighboring territories, and economic hardship. The Jews had resumed ceremonial worship according to God's law, but their hearts were not in it. They had expected more. They thought they deserved more.

Among this group of striving, struggling people, God continues to work his plan. This is the seed of Abraham he has covenanted to bless, and through whom he will bless all the families of the earth. He sends the leaders Ezra and Nehemiah, who most likely overlap in time with Malachi (and who address many of the same issues). He sends his word through Malachi, his faithful messenger—a word of rebuke for God's covenant people who aren't acting like it, but also a word of assurance that God's covenant promises will be accomplished. In general, *through Malachi the Lord reproves his self-righteous people, calling them to remember his covenant, seek him with their hearts, and prepare for his coming.* In these opening chapters, Malachi sets forth four of six main arguments through which the Lord rebukes his faithless people and calls them to honor him. Malachi's words can powerfully pierce the hearts of striving, struggling believers today.

DAY ONE—THE LORD WHO LOVES ISRAEL (MAL. 1:1–5)

1. From Malachi 1:1, what can we say about the message of this book? *Note: Remember that "Israel" was the name God gave to Jacob, Abraham's grandson and the father of the twelve sons/tribes of Israel (see Gen. 32:28–29). It was also the name of the northern kingdom (long gone). Here it refers to God's chosen people.*

2. The book of Malachi is organized into a series of six arguments. Look through the following generally recognized sections in order to identify for each the main issue presented by God and the contrarian response of the people (introduced by "But you say . . .").

   a. Malachi 1:2–5

   b. Malachi 1:6–2:9

   c. Malachi 2:10–16

   d. Malachi 2:17–3:5

   e. Malachi 3:6–12

   f. Malachi 3:13–4:3

3. The issue of the first argument (Mal. 1:2–5) is foundational: the love of God for his people, expressed in his choosing them for his own. Why might this weak remnant of Jews be doubting God's love? In what ways might you (or might some in the church today) be able to identify with this doubt?

4. God answers their doubt by affirming his sovereign covenant love for these descendants of Jacob, his chosen people. By contrast, God "hated" (i.e., determined *not* to choose) the descendants of Jacob's twin brother, Esau—eventually the nation of Edom. It may have appeared temporarily that Edom was favored, not having been destroyed by the Babylonians as Judah had been. But Malachi 1:3 applies a previous prophetic judgment of Jeremiah on Judah to *Edom*, showing that Edom in fact will be destroyed—and, unlike Judah, never restored (1:4). In 1:2–5, how would you sum up what God wants his people to understand?

5. The apostle Paul quotes Malachi in the process of explaining God's sovereignty in choosing those he will save and those he will not. In Romans 9:6–18, what do we learn of God's character and purposes? How does God's sovereign salvation lead us believers to rest in his love for us?

DAY TWO—PURE OR IMPURE OFFERINGS (MAL. 1:6–2:9)

1. In the second argument, the Lord accuses this people he loves (and the priests in particular) of despising his name. How? By offering impure sacrifices. Read the background in Leviticus 22:17–25.

   a. According to Malachi 1:6–2:3, how does the Lord view disobedience to these laws? Refer to particular verses in your answer.

b. Ceremonial laws about unblemished animals do not apply to us today; Christ the sinless Lamb has been sacrificed for us. But how do these laws speak to us today, teaching us about God and about how we should worship him?

2. In the midst of charging his people with dishonoring his name, God promises that his name will indeed be honored—in a big way. What is the message of Malachi 1:11, 14 (recall also Mal. 1:5; Zech. 14:9; 9:10; 8:20–23 . . . we could go farther back!)?

3. In Malachi 2:4–9, the Lord refers to his covenant with Levi—referring to the tribe of Levi to whom God's law entrusted temple-related duties. The priests (Levites descended from Moses's brother Aaron) offered sacrifices and taught the law to the people (see also Deut. 33:10). In what ways does Malachi contrast the qualities and the results of a faithful priest with those of an unfaithful one?

4. This rebuke of faithless worship and leaders of worship can both challenge and encourage us today, in the context of the church.

   a. How does Jesus Christ fulfill the description given in Malachi 2:5–7? (Consider verses such as John 8:25–32; Heb. 4:15.)

b. When we sinners put our faith in our sinless Savior
who offered himself as the perfect sacrifice for our
sin, how does he enable us to worship him truly
and forever? (Consider verses such as 2 Cor. 5:21;
1 Peter 2:4–5.)

c. How does this section of Malachi particularly challenge leaders and teachers in the church (and the
ones who support and listen to them)?

DAY THREE—FAITHFUL OR FAITHLESS
(MAL. 2:10–16)

1. In the third argument, the Lord charges this people
   he loves with faithlessness in relation to the marriage
   covenant.

   a. In Malachi 2:10–16, identify two kinds of faithless-
      ness among God's people (regarding marriage and
      divorce).

   b. A person's marital relationship is not disconnected
      from that person's relationship with God. In what
      ways is God joined to the marriage covenant accord-
      ing to Malachi 2:14–15, Genesis 2:21–24, and Mat-
      thew 19:3–9?

2. From Malachi 2:10–16, list some biblical reasons for faithfulness as opposed to faithlessness in regard to the marriage covenant.

3. How do we gain an even larger biblical perspective on the spiritual significance of the marriage covenant in Hosea 2:14–20, Ephesians 5:22–33, and Revelation 19:6–9?

4. Malachi's words about marriage speak powerfully to us today.

   a. Malachi twice admonishes God's people to "guard yourselves in your spirit" in order not to be faithless in relation to the covenant of marriage (Mal. 2:15–16). In what ways can we believers so guard ourselves?

b. In 1 Corinthians 7:1–16, what central goals are in view as Paul addresses the Corinthian church concerning this crucial area of life?

Day Four—The God of Justice (Mal. 2:17–3:5)

1. The fourth argument concerns the people's complaints about injustice, words that weary the Lord (Mal. 2:17). Why might the people in Malachi's time have been repeating such words? When have you perhaps heard— or spoken—words like these?

2. The Lord basically responds, *You want justice? Don't worry—it's coming. (I'm coming!) But are you ready?* Malachi 3:1 points ahead to two different messengers to come.

   a. First, in verse 1a, the Lord announces the messenger who will prepare the way for the Lord's coming. How is this messenger further identified in Malachi 4:5, Isaiah 40:3, and Matthew 11:7–15?

   b. Second, in verse 1b, "the Lord whom you seek" is identified as "the messenger of the covenant" who is coming! How do Matthew 3:1–3, Mark 1:1–3, and John 1:32–36 confirm the identity of this climactic divine messenger, the Lord Jesus?

3. Malachi looks ahead to the earth-shattering justice that Jesus Christ will bring, from his first to his final coming. To the question of who can endure the day of his coming, he gives two responses—first for those who *will* endure. In Malachi 3:2–4, what are the two vivid pictures of the purifying work accomplished in God's people, and what will be the result? (See also Zech. 13:9; 1 Peter 1:3–7; Rom. 12:1.)

4. But for those who do not belong to the Lord (Jews and non-Jews), his coming will bring only judgment. What can you observe in Malachi 3:5 about this judgment? How does this verse give a comprehensive picture of rejecting God?

Day Five—Review and Reflect

1. In what ways are we in the church today a lot like Israel in Malachi's time? Look back through Malachi 1:1–3:5: Which of these charges hits home in your heart? How often do you say a defensive "But . . ." (1:2, 6, 13; 2:14, 17)? Spend some moments of self-examination and repentance before the merciful Lord God, who has set his sovereign love on us in Christ.

2. The means of purifying our sinful hearts looms clearly in this final Old Testament book. Through the substitutionary death of God's divine messenger, God's promised perfect justice was accomplished. Through Christ's resurrection power in us, we are being transformed into his image. We will be able to endure that day, and to stand, only through Jesus our Savior. He will bring us through the refiner's fire, and we will shine like gold. Pray through the words of Titus 2:11–14. Write down phrases that stand out.

3. Look back through Malachi 1:1–3:5 to find the repeated name, "the LORD of hosts." Why might this name be especially comforting and strengthening to the postexilic remnant of Malachi's time? How does this name comfort and strengthen you today?

4. We said that in the book of Malachi *the Lord reproves his self-righteous people, calling them to remember his covenant, seek him with their hearts, and prepare for his coming.* How do these opening chapters encourage you in specific ways to grow in seeking the Lord who loves you, and to prepare today for that day of his coming?

Notes for Lesson 9

Lesson 10
(Mal. 3:6–4:6; Conclusion)

GOD POINTS US
TO THE COMING DAY

In the three postexilic prophets, we hear proclaimed with final boldness the dual prophetic themes of coming salvation for God's people and coming judgment for God's enemies. Malachi pulls these themes together emphatically, closing the Old Testament Scriptures with a sense of vibrant expectancy—expectancy fully met as the New Testament Scriptures open with the coming of Jesus.

We've seen Malachi's central thrust: through this prophet *the Lord reproves his self-righteous people, calling them to remember his covenant, seek him with their hearts, and prepare for his coming.* We've seen the organization of this book into six specific arguments in which the Lord offers his rebuke, hears the people's protesting response, and persistently calls them to follow him faithfully to the end. From the promises of purification and restoration, we know that there will be a final faithful remnant—in fact a final group of faithful worshipers drawn from all the nations of the world. This book addressed to Israel makes us pray for God's chosen ones both among the ethnic Jews and among the children of Abraham who are grafted into God's family by faith in his Son, our Savior.

Malachi's final chapters offer the last two arguments presented by God to a stubborn people, rebuking them and yet mercifully calling them to return to him and find blessing. The coming judgment is vivid and fearful, and yet the coming healing and joy for those who listen and turn to the Lord is great. We believers who look now for the Lord's second coming should feel this tension strongly as well, not only bearing in mind the impending final judgment but also longing for the appearing of our risen Savior who will make all things new. In the meantime, we often struggle. We're being refined by fire. We can't yet see the King. Malachi urges us to walk faithfully forward until we see his face.

DAY ONE—ABOUT THOSE TITHES (MAL. 3:6–12)

1. The fifth argument of Malachi brings a compassionate call to Israel (the "children of Jacob") based not on their goodness but on the Lord himself—his character and his covenant promises. List the qualities of God that shine from Malachi 3:6–7. (See also Zech. 1:3 and Hag. 2:17.) How does this repeated call well summarize the message of these prophets?

2. Malachi 3:7–9 includes two "Buts." How would you characterize the people's words here? According to the background in Deuteronomy 14:22–28, what kind of tithes did the Lord require, and for what purposes were these tithes used?

3. In what ways might Malachi 3:10–12 be misused, either then or now? In the context of this whole book, what would be the best way to seek and receive these promised blessings from God?

4. How does Malachi 3:10–12 show the overflowing nature of God's blessings? How does the broader biblical context illumine the depths of these blessings and the nature of our right response to them? See Genesis 12:1–4, Romans 8:32, and 2 Corinthians 9:6–15.

Day Two—God's Distinctions (Mal. 3:13–4:3)

1. Divide Malachi's sixth and final argument (Mal. 3:13–4:3) into three sections. For each section, summarize what is being said about the distinction between God's people and those who are not God's people.

2. Contrast the attitude of the ones God addresses in Malachi 3:13–15 with the attitude of those in verses 16–18. What words and phrases show how God looks on the second group? What does this mean to you today, as one who serves this Lord who does not change?

3. Again we are looking forward to the coming "day."

   a. In contrast with the "refiner's fire" (Mal. 3:2–3), we now see the fire of God's wrath: How does Malachi 4:1 show the power and extent of God's final punishment for those who are not his? (See also 2 Thess. 1:7–10.)

b. Read and meditate on the startling, beautiful contrast offered by Malachi 4:2–3. Write down and ponder the various vivid pictures through which we glimpse the full joy of our salvation.

4. Many people of faith have asked questions like the ones in Malachi 3:13–15 (compare Ps. 73:2–3; Hab. 1:13). How does this book show us the difference between asking these questions faithfully versus faithlessly? (See also Ps. 73:16–28; Hab. 3:17–19.)

DAY THREE—THE OLD TESTAMENT'S FINAL WORDS
(MAL. 4:4–6)

1. Read the book's conclusion (Mal. 4:4), and recall the scene with Moses alluded to (Ex. 19:1–6). How do this verse and that scene draw together the main concerns of this book?

2. In Malachi 4:5–6, Malachi brings to a climax his focus on the day of the Lord and the messengers that day will bring. Verse 5 calls the messenger of 3:1a "Elijah"; we have seen Jesus's direct identification of this figure as John the Baptist, who prepared the way before him (Matt. 11:7–14). How is Malachi's focus on this coming prophet a fitting end to the book and also a bridge between the Old and New Testaments (see also Luke 3:2–9)?

3. On the mountain of transfiguration, with Jesus appeared these same two figures, Moses and Elijah, representing all the Law and the Prophets (see Luke 9:28–36). They were talking with Jesus about his immanent "departure," or his "exodus" (Luke 9:31); that is, they were discussing his death on the cross. Think back through Malachi's themes in light of Jesus's death on the cross in the place of sinners; what are some ways in which these themes find their ultimate meaning as we look to Jesus?

4. The last verse of Malachi does not end with happy reso-
lution. What is the aching need expressed, one that is
ultimately addressed in the covenant community of the
people of God? What is the final fearsome warning?
How might this need and this warning help wake us up
to proclaim more faithfully the coming of Jesus, and to
look more faithfully to the day of his coming again?

DAY FOUR—REVIEW AND REFLECT ON MALACHI

1. God our loving Father looms lovingly over the whole
book of Malachi. The haunting final picture of fathers
and children brings back the Lord's voice telling Israel
that he loves them (Mal. 1:2) and that he is their father
(Mal. 1:6). Recall also Malachi 2:10 and 3:6–7, 17. How
does reconciliation with God our Father create a holy
covenant community? How do these truths lead you to
pray for your own family and church community?

2. The difference between the blaze of final judgment and the warmth of the sun's healing is in the "sun of righteousness" (Mal. 4:2)—in fact, the Son of God. How is Christ's righteousness our only hope? See 2 Corinthians 5:21; Philippians 3:7–11; I Peter 2:24–25. (Read all, but comment on only one.)

3. Malachi shows the battle between our words and God's Word. As you look back through the book, how is this true? And how does this battle perhaps rage in your own life and experience?

4. How gracious of God to send these words through Malachi to his people, to call them from faithless to faithful worship of the Lord, who would pour out blessing as they return to him! In what ways does this book encourage you to think and pray about your worship to God? See also Psalm 119:2, 10 and Romans 12:1–2.

Day Five—Review and Reflect on the Postexilic Prophets

1. Haggai, Zechariah, and Malachi spoke to a people who had been promised an eternal King on the throne of David (recall 2 Sam. 7:9–16). After the exile, their return to Jerusalem renewed their hope in God's promises. But their rebuilding turned out to be hard and long, and their king was nowhere in sight. They were a weak remnant, serving a foreign king and surrounded by enemies. These are good books for believers to read today, in these last days before Jesus comes again. Why? In what ways can we identify with this remnant and take the prophets' words deep into our hearts?

2. The historical context of Jerusalem, the temple, and the people of Israel is vivid and concrete in these books: God chose a real people in a real land to work his redemptive plan fulfilled in King Jesus, the Son of David. We have seen how the New Testament shows that fulfillment: those of faith in Christ are all sons of Abraham (Gal. 3:7–9), and the new Jerusalem of Revelation 21–22 is the promised place where God will dwell forever with his people (Rev. 21:3). However, the apostle Paul tells the Gentiles "grafted in" by faith not to be arrogant toward the Jewish branches broken off through lack of faith—but rather to be humble and aware of the kindness of God, looking for his mercy to those biological offspring of Abraham. Read Romans 11:17–24; how does it encourage you to pray?

3. Even with their focus on this one small territory of Judah, the postexilic prophets (in harmony with the entire Old Testament) look to a salvation that reaches all the nations of the earth; Jesus is King over all. Look back and find one or two verses from the books of Haggai, Zechariah, and Malachi that show God's far-reaching plan for all the nations. How do these verses lead you to pray and plan?

4. How, specifically, have these great prophets encouraged you to be faithful in small things as well as big ones (see Zech. 4:10)?

5. Praise God for the way the glory of his Son shines through all the Scriptures—and particularly through these books that close the Old Testament and reach toward the New. Pray through the following verses (and/or others), thanking God for the salvation accomplished through the promised King, who came, who died, who rose again, and who is coming again for us, his beloved people: Haggai 2:4–9; Zechariah 9:9–10 and 13:1; Malachi 3:1–3 and 4:2.

Notes for Lesson 10

Notes for Leaders

What a privilege it is to lead a group in studying the Word of God! Following are six principles offered to help guide you as you lead.

1. The Primacy of the Biblical Text

If you forget all the other principles, I encourage you to hold on to this one! The Bible is God speaking to us, through his inspired Word—living and active and sharper than a two-edged sword. As leaders, we aim to point people as effectively as possible into this Word. We can trust the Bible to do all that God intends in the lives of those studying with us.

This means that the job of a leader is to direct the conversation of a group constantly back into the text. If you "get stuck," usually the best thing to say is: "Let's go back to the text and read it again . . ." The questions in this study aim to lead people into the text, rather than into a swirl of personal opinions about the topics of the text; therefore, depending on the questions should help. Personal opinions and experiences will often enrich your group's interactions; however, many Bible studies these days have moved almost exclusively into the realm of "What does this mean to me?" rather than first trying to get straight on "What does this mean?"

We'll never understand the text perfectly, but we can stand on one of the great principles of the Reformation: the *perspicuity* of Scripture. This simply means *understandability*. God made us word-creatures, in his image, and he gave us a Word that he wants us to understand more and more, with careful reading and study, and shared counsel and prayer.

The primacy of the text implies less of a dependence on commentaries and answer guides than often has been the case. I do not offer answers to the questions, because the answers are in the biblical text, and we desperately need to learn how to dig in and find them. When individuals articulate what they find for themselves (leaders included!), they have learned more, with each of their answers, about studying God's Word. These competencies are then transferable and applicable in every other study of the Bible. Without a set of answers, a leader will not be an "answer person," but rather a fellow searcher of the Scriptures.

Helps *are* helpful in the right place! It is good to keep at hand a Bible dictionary of some kind. The lessons themselves actually offer context and help with the questions as they are asked. A few commentaries are listed in the "Notes on Translations and Study Helps," and these can give further guidance after one has spent good time with the text itself. I place great importance as well on the help of leaders and teachers in one's church, which leads us into the second principle.

2. THE CONTEXT OF THE CHURCH

As Christians, we have a new identity: we are part of the body of Christ. According to the New Testament, that body is clearly meant to live and work in local bodies, local churches. The ideal context for Bible study is within a church body—one that is reaching out in all directions to the people around it. (Bible studies can be the best places for evangelism!) I realize that these studies will be used in all kinds of ways and places; but whatever the context, I would hope that the group leaders have a layer of solid church leaders around them, people to whom they can go with questions and concerns as they study the Scriptures. When a leader doesn't know the answer to a question that arises, it's really OK to say, "I don't know. But I'll be happy to try to find out." Then that leader can go to pastors and teachers, as well as to commentaries, to learn more.

The church context has many ramifications for Bible study. For example, when a visitor attends a study and comes to know the Lord, the visitor—and his or her family—can be plugged into the context of the church. For another example, what happens in a Bible study often can be integrated with other courses of study within the church, and even with the preaching, so that the whole body learns and grows together. This depends, of course, on the connection of those leading the study with those leading the church—a connection that I have found to be most fruitful and encouraging.

3. The Importance of Planning and Thinking Ahead

How many of us have experienced the rush to get to Bible study on time . . . or have jumped in without thinking through what will happen during the precious minutes of group interaction . . . or have felt out of control as we've made our way through a quarter of the questions and used up three-quarters of the time!

It is crucial, after having worked through the lesson yourself, to think it through from the perspective of leading the discussion. How will you open the session, giving perhaps a nutshell statement of the main theme and the central goals for the day? (Each lesson offers a brief introduction that will help with the opening.) Which questions do you not want to miss discussing, and which ones could you quickly summarize or even skip? How much time would you like to allot for the different sections of the study?

If you're leading a group by yourself, you will need to prepare extra carefully—and that can be done! If you're part of a larger study, perhaps with multiple small groups, it's helpful for the various group leaders to meet together and to help each other with the planning. Often, a group of leaders meets early on the morning of a study in order to help the others with the fruit of their study, plan the group time, and pray—which leads into the fourth principle.

4. The Crucial Role of Prayer

If these words we're studying are truly the inspired Word of God, then how much do we need to ask for his Spirit's help and guidance as we study his revelation! This is a prayer found often in Scripture itself, and a prayer God evidently loves to answer: that he would give us understanding of his truth according to his Word. I encourage you as a leader to pray before and as you work through the lesson, to encourage those in your group to do the same, to model this kind of prayer as you lead the group time, to pray for your group members by name throughout the week, and to ask one or two "prayer warriors" in your life to pray for you as you lead.

5. The Sensitive Art of Leading

Whole manuals, of course, have been written on this subject! Actually, the four principles preceding this one may be most fundamental in cultivating your group leadership ability. Again, I encourage you to consider yourself not as a person with all the right answers, but rather as one who studies along with the people in your group—and who then facilitates the group members' discussion of all they have discovered in the Scriptures.

There is always a tension between pouring out the wisdom of all your own preparation and knowledge, on the one hand,

and encouraging those in your group to relish and share all they have learned, on the other. I advise leaders to lean more heavily toward the latter, reserving the former to steer gently and wisely through a well-planned group discussion. What we're trying to accomplish is not to cement our own roles as leaders, but to participate in God's work of raising up mature Christians who know how to study and understand the Word—and who will themselves become equipped to lead.

With specific issues in group leading—such as encouraging everybody to talk, or handling one who talks too much—I encourage you to seek the counsel of one with experience in leading groups. There is no better help than the mentoring and prayerful support of a wise person who has been there! That's even better than the best "how-to" manual. If you have a number of group leaders, perhaps you will invite an experienced group leader to come and conduct a practical session on how to lead.

Remember: the default move is, "Back to the text!"

6. THE POWER OF THE SCRIPTURES TO DELIGHT

Finally, in the midst of it all, let us not forget to delight together in the Scriptures! We should be serious but not joyless! In fact, we as leaders should model for our groups a growing and satisfying delight in the Word of God—as we notice its beauty, stop to linger over a lovely word or phrase, enjoy the poetry, appreciate the shape of a passage from beginning to end, laugh at a touch of irony or an image that hits home, wonder over a truth that pierces the soul.

May we share and spread the response of Jeremiah, who said:

Your words were found, and I ate them,
  and your words became to me a joy
  and the delight of my heart. (Jer. 15:16)

Outline of Haggai

In Haggai, the all-powerful Lord commands and helps his people not to falter in worshiping him to the very end, when through their line of promise God's glory will be revealed.

OUTLINE OF ZECHARIAH

Zechariah urged God's people to return to the Lord and to look in faith for the glorious plan of salvation to be accomplished through the coming King, who would restore Jerusalem in a greater way than they could imagine.

OUTLINE OF MALACHI

Through Malachi the Lord reproves his self-righteous people, calling them to remember his covenant, seek him with their hearts, and prepare for his coming.

   I. Introduction: The Oracle of the Word of the Lord (Mal. 1:1)
  II. Six Arguments for God's Contrarian People (Mal. 1:2–4:3)
      1. About God's Love for His Chosen People (1:2–5)
      2. About Offerings (1:6–2:9)
      3. About the Covenant of Marriage (2:10–16)
      4. About Justice (2:17–3:5)
      5. About Tithes and Blessing (3:6–12)
      6. About Present and Eternal Distinctions (3:13–4:3)
 III. Conclusion: Look for the Day of the Lord (Mal. 4:4–6)

Suggested
Memory Passages

Be strong, all you people of the land, declares the Lord. Work, for I am with you, declares the Lord of hosts, according to the covenant that I made with you when you came out of Egypt. My Spirit remains in your midst. Fear not.

Haggai 2:4b–5

Then he said to me, "This is the word of the Lord to Zerubbabel: Not by might, nor by power, but by my Spirit, says the Lord of hosts. Who are you, O great mountain? Before Zerubbabel you shall become a plain. And he shall bring forward the top stone amid shouts of 'Grace, grace to it!'"

Then the word of the Lord came to me, saying, "The hands of Zerubbabel have laid the foundation of this house; his hands shall also complete it. Then you will know that the Lord of hosts has sent me to you. For whoever has despised the day of small things shall rejoice."

Zechariah 4:6–10a

Behold, I send my messenger, and he will prepare the way before me. And the Lord whom you seek will suddenly come to his temple; and the messenger of the covenant in whom you delight, behold, he is coming, says the LORD of hosts. But who can endure the day of his coming, and who can stand when he appears? For he is like a refiner's fire and like fullers' soap. He will sit as a refiner and purifier of silver, and he will purify the sons of Levi and refine them like gold and silver, and they will bring offerings in righteousness to the LORD.

Malachi 3:1–3

NOTES ON TRANSLATIONS AND STUDY HELPS

This study can be done with any reliable translation of the Bible, although I recommend the English Standard Version for its essentially literal but beautifully readable translation of the original languages. In preparing this study, I have used and quoted from the English Standard Version, published by Crossway in Wheaton, Illinois.

These lessons are designed to be completed with only the Bible open in front of you. The point is to grapple with the text, not with what others have said about the text. The goal is to know, increasingly, the joy and reward of digging into the Scriptures, God's breathed-out words, which are not only able to make us wise for salvation through faith in Christ Jesus but also profitable for teaching, reproof, correction, and training in righteousness, that each of us may be competent, equipped for every good work (2 Tim. 3:15–17). To help you dig in, essential and helpful contexts and comments are given throughout the lessons.

Along with basic Bible handbooks, translations, and dictionaries easily available online, I have used and learned from the following books in my study and preparation; you may find sources such as these helpful at some point.

Barker, Kenneth L., and John R. Kohlenberger III, eds. *The Expositor's Bible Commentary: Old Testament.* Grand Rapids: Zondervan, 1994.

Boice, James Montgomery. *The Minor Prophets: An Expositional Commentary.* Vol. 2, *Micah–Malachi.* Grand Rapids: Baker Books, 2002.

Duguid, Iain M., and Matthew P. Harmon. *Zephaniah, Haggai, Malachi.* Reformed Expository Commentary Series. Phillipsburg, NJ: P&R Publishing, 2018.

ESV Study Bible. English Standard Version. Wheaton: Crossway, 2008.

McComiskey, Thomas Edward, ed. *The Minor Prophets: An Exegetical and Expository Commentary.* Vol. 3, *Zephaniah, Haggai, Zechariah, Malachi.* Grand Rapids: Baker Academic, 1998.

Phillips, Richard D. *Zechariah.* Reformed Expository Commentary Series. Phillipsburg, NJ: P&R Publishing, 2007.

Kathleen Nielson is an author and speaker who loves working with women in studying the Scriptures. She has taught literature (PhD, Vanderbilt University), directed women's Bible studies in local churches, and served as director of The Gospel Coalition's women's initiatives from 2010 to 2017. She and her husband, Niel, make their home partly in Wheaton, Illinois, and partly in Jakarta, Indonesia, where Niel helps to lead a network of Christian schools and universities. They have three sons, three daughters-in-law, and a growing number of grandchildren.